A GREAT WEEKEND IN

STOCKHOLM

A GREAT WEEKEND
IN
STOCKHOLM

Stockholm is the perfect destination, a small capital city that manages to combine the appeal of the traditional with the hunt for the trendy, the allure of urban sophistication with the simpler attractions of nature, and the best of 21st-century technology with the historic interest of centuries-old arts and crafts. It is home to the Nobel Prize and the latest in design, contemporary music and lifestyle. A city of contrasts, it is interesting and refreshing to see just how history, culture and the demands of modern life can co-exist successfully.

identity – clearly evident in the buildings, art and outlook of the city today. The Swedes are known to be remarkably open to new ideas and to be adventurous in their tastes and choices. It is no coincidence that Stockholm is often selected as the testing ground for new and innovative concepts, particularly in the field of information technology. You'll also find much of interest in the world of design – both interior and industrial – art, music and fashion, as well as ground-breaking projects to protect the environment and minimise our impact on the planet. And the Swedes certainly have a lot to be proud of in this respect. Two-thirds of the city is made up of natural environment, including the world's first city national park – the Royal Ekopark. Stockholm's 700,000 inhabitants don't have to put up with the degree of pollution that is common to so many of the world's cities today and can enjoy a diverse range of outdoor pursuits in the heart of the city. Popular activities include salmon fishing, camping in the local parks, skiing in the municipal gardens, swimming and

The foundations of the capital were lain by Birger Jarl in the 13th century, but archaeological evidence has shown that the Vikings settled and traded here from the 9th century. Many hundreds of years of history have shaped the character of Stockholm, from the fires that destroyed much of the town in the Middles Ages, to the building boom of the industrial revolution. The city has embraced artistic influences from France, Italy and Austria, while at the same time creating its own Swedish

walking, or taking picturesque boat rides on Lake Mälaren or along the archipelago formed by the first of the city's islands. Stockholm is interconnected by over 50 bridges, and boasts no fewer than 14 islands. The city is also a manageable size and can easily be explored by foot, bike or boat. The narrow streets of Gamla Stan,

the most of Stockholm's numerous restaurants, where the menus boast a fabulous mix of traditional Swedish cuisine and the latest in flavours and ingredients. Restaurants and cafés are also the best places to get to know the locals, who are very friendly. You'll find that the young people are very hip and

the glamorous and sweeping avenues of Östermalm, the modern and lively 'City' district and the somewhat bohemian and arty Södermalm area are among its many

highlights. The tree-lined paths in the Djurgården and Haga Park provide the perfect place for a walk and the royal palaces are a sight to behold. If it's culture you are after, there are plenty of museums and art galleries to keep you occupied, but if you'd prefer to check out the latest in Swedish chic – head for Södermalm and the city centre. Lovers of Swedish design will be in heaven, and foodies can make

trendy and hang out in the hottest clubs or the trendiest stores, as well as in the public parks and museums. Children have a special place in the hearts of the Swedish and tourists are made to feel very welcome. So for those who haven't got time to brush up on their Swedish, there's no need to panic, as the majority of Swedes speak excellent English and are only too happy to help out. Of course if that isn't enough to keep you going for a whole weekend, you can always leave the city centre behind and head off to explore what lies outside. You can take a traditional steamboat and visit some of

the 24,000 islands which make up the archipelago to the east of the city or spend a day at the magnificent home and gardens of the Royal family on the island of Lovön, less than an hour from the capital. Alternatively, if you just want to relax and put your feet up, you can treat yourself to a genuine Swedish massage or rejuvenate your tired muscles in an Art Nouveau-style spa, or a jacuzzi or sauna. The charms of Stockholm are many, chances are you'll find more than one.

How to get there

THE CLIMATE

Stockholm's climate is not as obvious as you might think. The winter is long and cold, with heavy snowfalls and temperatures dropping as low as -7°C (19°F), but the days can often be dry and clear. The sunlight hours can be bright and luminous, with the sun reflecting off the snow. Come the end of September, the days get shorter, with daylight lasting from 9am to 3pm in the depths of winter. The days start to get longer from the beginning of April, with summer only really lasting for the months of June and July (the latter being the traditional holiday month in Sweden). The temperature can reach 20-25°C (68-77°F) or even warmer, when the sky is clear and cloudless, but it can also change dramatically during the course of a day. The sea surrounds the city and clouds form with the merest whiff of wind, so it's worth taking a light sweater or windproof jacket, as well as an umbrella when you go out.

WHEN TO GO

Spring and summer are the best seasons to visit Stockholm, when the city resembles a seaside resort and locals take every opportunity to lie around on the grass and make the most of the sun. It does not get dark until 11pm but even then there is a kind of half-light during which the sun remains just below the horizon, eventually rising around 4am, which can be a little disconcerting. If you're a light sleeper, remember to pack an eye mask as bedrooms can be quite light in the early hours. December, when the Swedish are busy with their traditional Christmas preparations, is also a good time to visit Stockholm, when the city is lively and atmospheric. Some tour operators have special offers for weekend trips between October and March – so it's worth checking out discount deals before booking.

GETTING THERE

If you are planning to spend a weekend, even a long one, in Stockholm, the quickest and indeed cheapest option is to fly. Prices for air travel to Sweden have been dropping recently and it is worth looking in the classified sections of the Sunday newspapers for special offers. Taking the car is possible, with ferries operating from Newcastle to Gothenburg, for example, but do bear in mind the high cost of petrol in Sweden. The train from London to Stockholm takes around 25 hours and is more expensive than flying. You will probably have to change four or five times. The bus is not only rather gruelling but is unlikely to be cheaper than a discounted flight.

FLIGHTS FROM THE UK

The following companies operate flights from the UK to Stockholm:

British Airways
☎ 0845 7733377
www.british-airways.com

Flights daily from Heathrow and Gatwick.

Finnair
☎ 020 7408 1222
www.finnair.com
Flights daily from Manchester to Stockholm.

KLM UK
☎ 0870 507 4074
www.klmuk.com
Regular flights from UK regional airports to Stockholm via Amsterdam.

Maersk Air
☎ 020 7333 0066
www.maersk-air.com

Ryanair
☎ 0870 333 1250
www.ryanair.com
Flights from Stansted to Stockholm Skavsta and Vasteras airports.

Scandinavian Airlines
☎ 0845 6072 7727
www.sas.se
Flights from Heathrow, Stansted, Edinburgh and Manchester.

Virgin Express
☎ 020 7744 0004
www.virginexpress.com
Flights from London Heathrow to Stockholm Arlanda airport.

FROM THE REPUBLIC OF IRELAND

Finnair are the only airline offering direct flights to Sweden, with daily services (except Wednesday) from Dublin to Stockholm:

☎ 01 844 6565
www.finnair.com

FROM THE USA AND CANADA

For those travelling from North America, there are a number of operators with direct flights to Stockholm. Others go via different European cities. Here are a few of the options:

Delta Airlines
☎ 1 800 241 4141
www.delta-air.com
Direct flights from New York to Stockholm.

Finnair
☎ 1 800 461 8651
www.finnair.com
Flights from New York via Helsinki and from Toronto via Helsinki (summer only).

Icelandair
☎ 1 800 223 5500
www.icelandair.com
Flights to Stockholm via
Reykjavik from New York,
Minneapolis, Baltimore,
Boston, Orlando and Halifax.

Scandinavian Airways (SAS)
☎ 1 800 221 23 50 (tollfree
from US and Canada)
www.flysas.com or www.sas.se
Direct flights daily from New
York and Chicago and flights
from Seattle via Copenhagen.

FROM AUSTRALIA AND NEW ZEALAND
There are no direct flights
from Australia or New
Zealand to Sweden. Travellers
must fly to a gateway city in
Europe or Asia and take a
connecting flight. It's worth
heading to London,
Amsterdam or Frankfurt first
to take advantage of the
cheaper onward flights.

PACKAGE TOURS FROM THE UK
A number of companies offer
inclusive packages for city
breaks with a range of
accommodation.

The following are a selection
of tour operators:

Abercrombie & Kent
☎ 0845 0700 610
www.abercrombiekent.co.uk

Scantours
☎ 020 7839 2927
www.scantours.co.uk

Specialised Tours
☎ 01342 712785
www.specialisedtours.com

FROM AIRPORT TO CITY CENTRE

Most international and
domestic flights arrive at
Arlanda airport (☎ 08 797
61 00), located 45km
(31 miles) north of Stockholm.
There's a choice of transport
into the city centre:

Fastest: high-speed trains to
Stockholm's Central Station
leave every 10-15 minutes
from the Arlanda Express
station, located beneath the
airport. The journey takes 20
minutes and tickets (120kr)
can be purchased from ticket
machines or

SWEDISH EMBASSIES ABROAD

Australia
Turrana Street
Yarralumla, ACT
☎ 06 270 2700

Canada
377 Dalhousie Street
Ottawa, Ontario K1N 9NB
☎ 613 241 8553

New Zealand
Consulate General
13th Floor, Aitken Street
Thordon, Wellington
☎ 04 499 9895

Republic of Ireland
Sun Alliance House
13-17 Dawson Street
Dublin 2
☎ 01 671 5822

UK
11 Montagu Place
London W1H 2AL
☎ 020 7724 2101
www.swedish-embassy.org.uk/
embassy

US
1501 M Street NW
Washington DC 20005
☎ 202 467 2600

LEV information centres at the airport.

Most economical: the airport buses, Flygbussarna, leave every 10 minutes and take around 40 minutes to reach the bus station, adjacent to the Central Station. Tickets cost 70kr and can be purchased on the bus (credit cards accepted). You can ask the driver to book a taxi to take you from the station to your hotel. You need to pay the bus driver who will then give you a token for the taxi driver. If you are heading to the centre the fare will be around 100kr, including luggage.

Most expensive: if you have lots of luggage, a taxi is an alternative option, albeit a rather expensive one, but if you are in a group it could be more economical. There are fixed rate fares: 350kr to the airport from the city centre and 450kr for the return journey (credit cards accepted). Make sure you

choose a vehicle that operates this fixed rate before you get in. Prices are usually displayed in the back window.

From Skavsta airport (located 100km/62 miles south of the city), airport coaches (*Flyg-bussarna*) ferry passengers directly to Stockholm Cityterminal, while at Vasteras (105km/65 miles west of the city) there are high speed rail links taking only 50 minutes.

CAR HIRE

Hiring a car is not advisable for those intending to spend all their time in Stockholm itself. Excursions to Drottningholm and the archipelago can be enjoyed by boat. The speed limit for cars is 50km/h (30mph) and the traffic is not too heavy, but hiring a car is not really necessary in a city of Stockholm's size. If you do want to hire a vehicle, try one of the following international companies:

Avis: ☎ 020 78 82 00
www.avis.com

Budget: ☎ 020 78 77 87
www.budget.com

Hertz: ☎ 020 21 12 11
www.hertz.com

Hire companies often have special weekend deals. You can also rent cars at reasonable prices from Statoil petrol stations (open 9.30am-5pm).

VISAS

US, Canadian, Australian and New Zealand citizens only need a valid passport to enter Sweden and can stay for up to three months.

CUSTOMS

You must be aged over 20 to bring alcohol into Sweden. Visitors from the EU can bring in one litre of spirits, 3 litres of wine and 15 litres of strong beer, as well as 300 cigarettes/ 150 cigarillos/75 cigars/400g of leaf tobacco, provided the

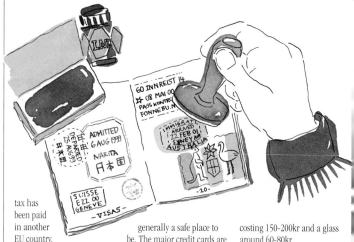

tax has been paid in another EU country.

The tax-free limits for non-EU citizens are one litre of spirits, 2 litres of wine, 15 litres of beer, 200 cigarettes/100 cigarillos/50 cigars/250g leaf tobacco, 50g perfume, 500g coffee and 100g tea.

CURRENCY

The Swedish currency is the krona (abbreviated as kr, krs or sek), made up of 100 öre. It comes in coins of 50 öre, 1kr, 5kr and 10kr and notes of 20kr, 50kr, 100kr, 500kr, 1000kr and 10,000kr. The exchange rate against other currencies will of course vary – at the time of going to press 1kr was worth around €0.11. The best place to change money is at the yellow Forex offices, which can be found in the city centre and at Arlanda airport and the Central Station. You can also change money in post offices sporting the Växel (exchange) sign. It is always safer to carry your money as traveller's cheques rather than large amounts of cash, although Stockholm is

generally a safe place to be. The major credit cards are accepted almost everywhere and there are plenty of ATMs for withdrawing cash.

If you lose your credit card phone the following numbers:

Visa: ☎ 020 79 31 46

American Express: ☎ 08 429 54 29

Mastercard: ☎ 020 79 13 24

Diners: ☎ 08 14 68 78

BUDGET

Prices in Stockholm are relatively high, in line with those of London, if not higher. The Swedish enjoy a high standard of living, as you will soon notice. There are not many hotels in Stockholm so they are always busy, and therefore quite expensive. Eating and drinking is likely to take up a large part of your budget. Prices in restaurants vary, of course, with dinner costing between 200-300kr in a top establishment and around 100kr for a set lunch. Wine will push the prices up dramatically, with a bottle

costing 150-200kr and a glass around 60-80kr.

Designer clothes cost the same as in other cities, but Swedish labels can be surprisingly affordable, so leave some room in your suitcase for some impulse purchases.

LANGUAGE

Swedish is a Germanic language and related to English, rather like French is related to Italian. It is in fact quite an easy language for

USEFUL NUMBERS AND WEBSITES

Swedish Travel and Tourism Council
5 Upper Montagu Street
London W1H 2AG
☎ 0800 3080 3080
📠 0207 724 5872

PO Box 4649
Grand Central Station
New York
NY 10163-4649
☎ 212 885 9700
📠 212 885 9764

www.visit-sweden.com
www.swetourism.se
www.stockholmtown.com

English speakers to pick up, but don't worry, most Swedes speak excellent English, particularly the youngsters. They are taught English at school and perfect it through watching television – films and TV series are generally shown in the original language. Swedish has three extra vowels (å, ä and ö), placed at the end of the alphabet – remember this when you are looking up street names on a map.

HOLIDAYS AND FESTIVALS

From 1-6 January (Epiphany), Good Friday, Easter Monday, 1 May (Labour Day), Ascension Day, Whit Monday, Midsummer's Eve (always on a Friday) and Midsummer's Day (the Saturday closest to the summer solstice). All Saints' Day is celebrated on the Saturday that falls between 31 October and 6 November and Christmas festivities take place on 25 and 26 December, although some shops and

businesses close on 24 December also, or at least shut their doors early. Other festivals include St Lucia's Day (13 December), Swedish National Day (6 June) and Walpurgis Night or *Valborgsmässoafton* (30 April). Nobel Prize Day is marked by ceremonies in Sweden on 10 December.

HEALTH

No vaccinations are required for Sweden; if you should fall ill, ask the hotel staff to find you a designated doctor. EU nationals can take advantage of Sweden's health service under the same terms as the residents of the country. You will need to take a completed E111 form with you (available in post offices in the UK) and show it when asking for medical treatment. A consultation in a medical centre or hospital clinic costs 120kr, whereas an appointment with a consultant will set you back 240kr. The doctor will give you a prescription to take to the

pharmacy (*apotek*). Citizens of non-EU countries will be charged for medical services, and it is wise to take out travel insurance. In the case of an emergency, go to the nearest hospital (with your passport and E111 form if applicable) where you will be treated. The casualty department is known as *Akutmottagning* in Swedish.

LOCAL TIME

Sweden conforms to Central European Time (always one hour ahead of Britain and Ireland). For most of the year, Sweden is six hours ahead of New York, nine hours behind Sydney and eleven hours behind Auckland. Clocks go forward by an hour in March and back by an hour in late October (on the same day as in Britain and Ireland).

VOLTAGE

The electricity supply is 220V and plugs have two round pins, so make sure you take an adaptor if you want to use any equipment.

SWEDISH DESIGN – COMBINING FORM WITH FUNCTION

Design is not just a creative or commercial activity in Sweden – it is part of the national psyche, dating back to the 1950s when Scandinavian functionalism conquered the United States, after making its mark at home. After several less artistically frenetic decades, a new generation of talent has pushed Sweden to the forefront of the international design world once more.

THE HISTORY OF SWEDISH DESIGN

'Everyday beauty', form and function characterise the spirit of Swedish design, the origins of which lie in the true spirit of democracy during which the state wanted all households to enjoy the same levels of comfort. The premise for this 'social design' dates back to the Universal Exhibition of 1897, where the very best of the applied arts were brought together in Stockholm. One of those represented was the artist Carl Larsson, whose watercolours of the interior of his Sundburn villa were shown for the first time. They depict simple rooms decorated with pale wooden furniture and fabrics designed by his wife Karin. Their light colours and rustic features were in strong contrast with the heavy and dark interiors of other artists. The author Ellen Key was inspired by his work to write *Beauty in the Home* in 1887, and two years later she formulated her social stance on design in

The David Design concept store

Beauty for All. Another author, historian and director of the Svenska Slöjd-föreningen (see p. 61), Gregor Paulsson,

Chair designed by Carl Malmsten

also helped to promote equality in Scandinavian design, and in 1919, his book *More Beautiful Everyday Objects* was published and became one of the main inspirations for the Stockholm Exhibition of 1930. Paulsson had radical theories on art and its social background, and made the case for well-designed objects for all classes in society. The book highlighted the trend towards designing more attractive and practical everyday objects.

Design Torget

PIONEERS OF SWEDISH DESIGN

Sweden was one of the strongholds of the Functional movement, whose breakthrough came with the Stockholm Exhibition, conceived by Gregor Paulsson in conjunction with the architect Gunnar Asplund, whose simple but sophisticated architecture received much attention outside Sweden at the time. The popular wooden furniture designed by Bruno Mathsson explored organic, even anthropomorphic shapes and he inspired many with his steel chairs with woven webbed seats. His 1934 'Eva' chair was very popular and has remained an enduring icon, as has his later 'Pernilla' design, which aimed to make the chair an even more comfortable tool for the home. The more classic designs of Josef Frank and Carl Malmsten were also shown at the 1930 exhibition. Frank was an Austrian architect living in Stockholm and father of the Swedish modern style inspired by the Biedermeier school. He was to become a legend of the Svenkst Tenn company, while Malmsten was a craftsman in wood, combining the rustic with the functional to wide acclaim.

CONQUERING THE WORLD OF DESIGN

In 1954, the Design in Scandinavia exhibition began its influential three-year tour of the United States, during which Scandinavian design became the model for the 'American Way of Life'. In 1955, the H55 Exhibition was held in Helsingborg, and saw the emergence of a number of inventive and talented Swedish designers responding to the new demands of the time, producing many original designs, among them the first household appliances (thanks to the Electrolux company).

A SOCIAL VISION

The 1970s and 80s saw the development of Sweden's social conscience in design terms, with the Ergonomi Design Gruppen producing furniture for the

IKEA — A GIANT IN DESIGN

The 1970s and 80s witnessed the dramatic expansion of Ikea. Formed in 1943, this Swedish furniture company explored the concept of 'beauty for all'. It combined this functionalist trend with acute commercial sense to become an innovative and internationally successful company, selling simple but charming designs with a personal touch. It now has 150 stores throughout the world and commissions independent designers to create collections that can be as unusual as they are innovative, in some cases harking back to the Gustavian era.

disabled and elderly. The designs ranged from daily household items to paramedic equipment, some of which, including the famous Fiskars scissors, became international bestsellers. The permanent exhibition, 1900-2000, One Hundred Years of Swedish Design, can be seen in the National Art Museum (see p. 61) and features products from the Ergonomi studio, along with highlights from the different stages in Swedish design.

Large industrial groups such as Volvo, Saab and Electrolux, also display the ergonomic concepts at the heart of their research and development.

'WINTRY' DESIGNS

Many Swedish designers successfully combine old references with new materials, and go beyond the confines of the 'social and universal' imposed for so long by the state. They preserve a sense of aestheticism with the everyday, the utilitarian and the functional. Often inspired by nature, contemporary Swedish design is sometimes described as 'wintry' due to the colours of the materials used, its simplicity, its humour and its uncomplicated poetry. Individual identity, however, is always apparent.

JONAS BOHLIN

Jonas Bohlin was the first to cause ripples on the waters of conformism. In 1982 his work

was exhibited at the graduation show at Konstfack, the National College of Arts, Craft and Design in Stockholm, and his 'Concrete' chair, made from steel and concrete, caused quite a stir. It was both a piece of sculpture

in an artistic installation and the epitome of Swedish post-modernist design. Jonas Bohlin continues to tread the fine line between art and design and remains an important influence with a strong personality. You can see more of his work in the gallery he opened in 2000 in Södermalm (see p. 48). He has also changed the face of a number of restaurants in Stockholm, such as Sturehof (see p. 82), Rolf Kök (see p. 80) and the legendary Riche (see p. 82). Rolf Kök (Rolf's Kitchen) was designed jointly with Thomas Sandell and was

Mies van der Rohe, Gropius and Aalto), Sandell describes himself as a 'maximalist', declaring 'minimalism'

The Kantin Moneo café

among the first mature examples of restaurant and bar design to transform the nightlife of the 1990s. Its style is sometimes described as 'Nordic Shaker'.

THOMAS SANDELL

Bohlin and Sandell, architect, international star and one of the most sought-after representatives of the latest developments in Swedish modernism, often worked together. Spiritual son of the masters of classical modernism (Le Corbusier,

somewhat dull. His style is characterised by discreet luxury and a sense of optimism, and his work can be seen in various interiors (see Kantin Moneo, the café in the Museum of Modern Art, p. 61), including a number of restaurants and suites in the Hotel Birger Jarl (see p. 76). He designs furniture, rugs, and individual items for the biggest names in Sweden (Asplun, Källemo and Ikea) and Italy (B&B, Cappellini). Other contemporary colleagues to have received international

acclaim include Mats Theselius, Björn Dahltröm, Jonas Lindwall, Pia Törnell and the trio of architects – Claesson-Koivisto-Rune. They all remain faithful to a Swedish tradition of simplicity and clarity, combined with a touch of cunning, humour and ingeniousness.

Birger Jarl Hotel

pale wood and artistic touches (not to mention designer photos of chips). The very pleasant Birger Jarl Hotel (see p. 76) has been renovated and offers a 'designer weekend', which includes not only the price of the room, but free entry to the main museums and reductions in some of the designer shops.

THE HEIGHT OF DESIGN

There are many shops and distributors who vie to present the best in contemporary Swedish design, including Asplund (see p. 100), Klara (see p. 46), Design House (see p. 100), Design Torget (see p. 101). The David Design concept store (see p. 103), opened in 2000 by David Carlsson, has a wonderful selection of goods from

household items to CDs. The large outlets, NK and Åhléns (see p. 104) also devote shelves to the latest in Swedish design, such as Inox Hackman's wonderful utensils.

STYLE, STYLE, STYLE

You don't have to go far to see fine examples of Swedish design – style is synonymous with Stockholm. Even the McDonald's in Kungsgatan has a Swedish interior with

Rugs designed by Asplund

Bonfires, festivals and fireworks

The Swedes are very attached to their national traditions, particularly those that involve a party and offer the opportunity to sing, dance, drink and eat. Their festivals are mostly organised around the seasons and religious occasions (the official religion is Protestantism). The highlight of the year is the Midsummer festival when the whole country celebrates.

Farewell winter

On 30 April, the eve of Walpurgis Night or *Valbörgs-massoaften*, the Swedes welcome the arrival of spring, lighting bonfires and singing celebratory songs. The choirs, mostly male, herald the return of sunny days (even if it's raining!). School leavers fill the streets, wearing their white hats to show that they have successfully graduated with a diploma.

St John's day

This rural festival, a celebration of fertility, is still alive and well in Sweden and offers the locals yet another chance to enjoy themselves in the open air. The Midsummer celebration (Midsommar) takes place during the weekend closest to the 24th of June, when darkness doesn't really fall and the midnight sun is in the north. Huge bonfires are built, people dance, visit friends and relatives, and maypoles are erected. Sometimes carpets of brightly coloured flowers replace the bonfires and the locals dance around them in a lively and spirited manner.

Crayfish parties in the moonlight

These celebrations take place throughout August and are held across the country by the light of the moon, to bid a wistful farewell to the all too short Swedish summer. This 100-year-old tradition was introduced by the government as a way of stopping all fishing until autumn. The very existence of the crayfish, which once thrived in the local lakes, was threatened

by huge exports made to top restaurants in Paris, Berlin and London, and they almost vanished from Swedish waters. Today, dining on crayfish is an important part of this folk ritual, in which plates bearing images of shellfish and lamps decorated with a waning moon are used. The crayfish used in the celebrations today are imported from Spain or the United States.

WAITING FOR CHRISTMAS

The Christmas period and the four weeks of Advent leading up to it are traditionally a very special time in the Swedish calendar, when people come together to enjoy a wonderful festive meal – an elaborate and more luxurious version of the traditional *smörgåsbord* (see p. 24). The days leading up to Christmas are among the longest and darkest of the year, but the locals make up for this with the light of thousands of candles flickering in the windows in celebration of St Lucia's Day (December 13). It is so cold outside that the celebrations mostly take place indoors, with homes warmly decorated with wreaths, angels and spicy gingerbread houses. The streets outside are ablaze with lights, and every family has

an Advent crown with four candles, one of which is lit on each of the Sundays leading up to Christmas. The first candle marks the start of the celebrations, which include a festive dinner and the giving of presents on the evening of Christmas Eve, generally accompanied by a humorous or ironic poem for each recipient. Mass is held at 7pm on 25 December.

ST LUCIA'S CROWN

St Lucia's Day is without doubt the most Swedish of traditions. Celebrations for the 'Day of Light' (13 December) begin in the morning. A young girl, chosen to be St Lucia, makes her way through the streets wearing a long white robe with a red sash and a crown of candles (or battery-powered lights) in her hair. She is accompanied by her maids of honour and sings traditional refrains, whilst carrying coffee and sweet saffron buns. In the larger towns the tradition is celebrated within the family unit. The mother prepares a tray with coffee and cake to be carried by the youngest member of the family (playing the role of St Lucia) to the father of the house, whilst he is still asleep.

STOCKHOLM'S GREEN SPACES

The Swedish are known to be very ecologically aware and everyone gets involved in protecting the environment. Sweden is principally a land of forests and lakes – half the country is covered in forests and there are no fewer than 100,000 lakes. Although it is the capital city with a population of 1.6 million, over two thirds of the city is made up of parks, woodlands and water.

CLEAN, FRESH WATER

Stockholm has no difficulty living up to its nickname of 'Beauty on the Water'. Whether it's fresh- or saltwater, there is certainly no shortage of the stuff. Built on 14 islands, where the freshwater of Lake Mälaren meets the brackish Baltic waves, the city is a paradise for nature lovers. Despite the currents, the seawater never makes its way into the lakes, even at the Gamla Stan meeting point. Travelling around Stockholm inevitably involves crossing a number of bridges, each one offering magnificent views of the city, and the water is so clean that you can often spot anglers tickling salmon. The local tap water is drawn from the Mälaren and Bornsjön lakes, as no industrial waste ever flows into them. Not only is it drinkable, but the tap water is also served with pride in the city's restaurants and cafés.

A SPOT OF BOATING

If you're visiting Stockholm during the summer, a boat trip is a must, even if it's only for a quick trip around the city, an

excursion to Drottningholm, the 17th-century royal residence located right on the lakeside (see pp. 72-73), or a tour of the stunning archipelago. The latter, a summer paradise for holidaymakers, is made up of an astonishing 24,000 islands, islets and rocks, which are easily accessible from the city centre. Escaping city dwellers own holiday homes here and enjoy fishing, swimming, watersports and the great outdoors. It doesn't take much to fall in love with this area.

BEAUTIFUL PARKS AND GARDENS

You're never far from a park in Stockholm. The city is proud to be home to the world's first urban national park, where you can fish and swim just minutes from the centre. Ecoparken surrounds the Brunnsviken bay to the north of Stockholm and is made up of the royal park of Djurgården, Ladugårdsgärdet, Norra Djurgården and Hagaparken. There are

gardens dotted all over the city and many have *parklekar*, where children can use toys and bicycles free of charge. Whilst some inhabitants grow vegetables in their own kitchen gardens city-style, others buy the organically grown produce from the gardens and greenhouses of Rosendals, in the heart of the Djurgården park (see p. 64).

EXPLORING ON FOOT OR BY BIKE

One of the great attractions of Stockholm is its very manageable size. People can walk or cycle almost everywhere, and bicycles left

them, although there are few of these anyway, and cars never block the cycle route. Drivers stop at red lights and pedestrians are very careful when crossing the road. At major intersections, the lights are accompanied by a series of sounds, which you will soon get used to – slow for green and fast for red.

SUNSHINE AND SEA

As soon as the first rays of sun emerge the locals head for the outdoors; on sunny days the beaches are awash with families enjoying the clean, pure waters of Lake Mälaren. The most popular beaches

the word, but rather pebble-covered stretches of land at the edge of the sea. In the winter months, the bravest locals break the ice and take a dip in the freezing waters. Not something recommended for the fainthearted!

outside for a few hours will still be in exactly the same place when you return. The locals respect the rules of the road to the letter and bicycle lanes are sacrosanct – scooters and mopeds stay clear of

include Smedsuddsbadet at the edge of Mariebergsparken, Rålambshovparken beach on the island of Kungsholmen and Långholmensstrandbad on Långholmen. They are not beaches in the true sense of

IN THE DAYS OF THE VIKINGS

Although the Swedish no longer summon their Viking gods – Thor and Odin – they still retain a certain pride about their distant ancestors, who were intrepid voyagers, merciless conquerors and adventurous traders. Even if Stockholm was not exactly the cradle for the fearless Vikings, the city and the surrounding area still bear the marks of its glorious if bloody past.

THE REIGN OF TERROR

The Vikings were a very determined lot, bent on achieving their one ambition – the acquisition of land and wealth through trade, raid, pillage or war – at any cost. Their reign of terror lasted more than two centuries (from around AD 800 to AD 1050), as they rampaged through conquered lands.

Whilst their Danish and Norwegian counterparts headed west, the Swedish Vikings focused on the east. Travelling back up the rivers that flowed into the Baltic Sea, they made their way into what is now Russia, where they settled and traded. They then pressed on to the Caspian Sea where they established important trading links with the Byzantine Empire and the Arab kingdoms, even making it as far as Baghdad.

BIRKA, THE VIKING TOWN

Sweden's oldest town, Birka, is situated on the island of Björkö (meaning 'the island of birches'), and was a Viking trading centre during its heyday in the 10th century. The Swedish Vikings also laid down their roots in Hovgården, on the island of Adelsö, and in the area to the north of Stockholm around Sigtuna and Uppsala. Birka features on the UNESCO World Heritage List, and was the first known anchorage point for the Swedish Vikings in around AD 760. It was from here that the merchant pirates set off on their long sea voyages. Birka's Viking museum was opened in 1996 and displays a fine collection of historical artefacts as well as scale models of the harbour

THE SVEA VIKING

To find out more about the seafaring Vikings, take a trip aboard the Svea Viking, a replica of an authentic *drakkar* (Viking longship). You can enjoy a 2-hour trip around the archipelago, admire the ingenious equipment that allowed the Vikings to cope with huge storms and navigate their intended route. The boat leaves daily at 11am, 2pm, 5pm and 7pm from the Skeppsbrokajen quay on Gamla Stan.

and craftsmen's quarters. It's a 2½-hour boat trip from the Stadhusbron quay near the town hall. For further information and timetables, contact: ☎ 08 789 24 90.

AT HOME WITH THE VIKINGS

Not all Vikings went out on expeditions. Most of them were farmers and craftsmen, as shown by the host of artefacts uncovered in various archeological sites. They

raised cattle, poultry and pigs, grew wheat, peas and onions and made butter, cream and cheese. Their craftsmen made combs, worked in bronze or created woven fabrics. Trading was in their blood, as the coins and treasure housed in

the basement of the History Museum (Historiska Museet) in Östermalm, bear witness (see p. 52).

EQUALITY OF THE SEXES

Not famous for their good manners, the Vikings were nonetheless early proponents of equal opportunity. Women were mistresses of their domain – the home – but were also in charge of the fields and the trading business when the men were away hunting or fishing. They had the right to choose their own husband and could even demand a divorce if they so desired. Perhaps this independent spirit has filtered through the generations to the young Swedish women of today.

THE END OF THE VIKINGS

In AD 830, Ansgar, a Benedictine monk, arrived from the Carolingian

kingdom to bring Christianity to the Swedish pagans. He baptised many of the Birka villagers, and it became a Christian community, with pagans and Christians living alongside each other quite happily until the end of the 10th century. The Vikings eventually left Birka and moved to Sigtuna, finally disappearing with the evangelisation of Europe and the advent of feudalism.

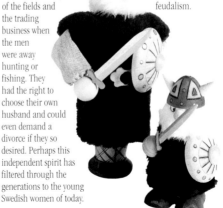

SWEDISH FASHION AND BEAUTY

The Swedes are past masters of relaxed, but up-to-the minute fashion. In the shadow of the clothing giant H&M, a new young generation of independent designers has created a 'made in Stockholm' look that is doing well in the fashionable boutiques of New York, London and Paris. Beauty is very important to the Swedes, and they take great care of their bodies and appearance.

Anna Holtblad

A SWEDISH IMPRINT

In Sweden, the prêt-à-porter range at H&M is pretty much known off by heart, but Swedish fashion doesn't stop there. After decades of politically correct design, a new generation of stylists has been making its mark over the last three years. Most of them were trained at the Beckmans School of Design (see p. 13), and their designs are highly trendy and very individual. During the 1980s and 1990s,

certain, now famous names, began to establish themselves: Filippa K, whose style was simple, conservative and humorous, and Anna Holtblad, who took Swedish knitwear beyond the traditional folk patterns. More recently, Johan Lindeberg has brought out his own funky label for men. Other important names in 21st-century Swedish fashion include Tiger, Acne Jeans and Paul & Friends. They are known internationally for their successful combination of style with comfort – as demanded by the locals.

NEWCOMERS ON THE SCENE

Recently, young outsiders, including Roland Hjört, have joined

the ranks of the Swedish fashion scene. In 1998, Hjört launched his own brand of jeans and T-shirts known as Whyred. Four trendy new names appeared in 2000 with their comfortable but sexy ranges of clothes – Marina Kereklidou, Lovisa Burfitt, Carin Rodebjer and Sara von Ehrenheim. Johan Schalin has also added his own original touch to the world of fashion, designing and making his own clothes in a boutique-studio in Kungsholmen. As early as 1995, years before the big New York buyers showed interest in the new young Swedish designers, Ulrika Nilsson opened her shop Jus on the Birgerjarlsgatan, offering a valuable distribution facility. Her shop is

definitely worth a visit, along with Torget Mode's two outlets, one in the city centre and another in Södermalm (see p. 90). Here new designers, many of them unknown, hire sections of a communal shop to display their designs.

NATURAL BEAUTY

Blonde hair, blue eyes and fair, peach-like skin isn't just a cliché, it's simply the way that most Swedes look. Young Swedes, in particular, are very much into the cult of the body beautiful and are preoccupied not so much with outward appearances as with internal well-being and health. They practise their favourite sports regularly, ride around on bicycles, take part in the Stockholm marathon and enjoy skating in the winter months. On the whole, Swedes tend to look after their bodies much more than other nations.

WATER

Water is a quintessential part of the Swedish psyche, and Swedes love to spend weekends enjoying water-based activities, not to mention hiring a pool or sauna for an evening party. A love of water is instilled in children from their earliest days, and every swimming pool here is equipped with its own infant pool. There are certainly some lovely baths to visit in Stockholm, including the Centralbadet (p. 59) and the Sturebadet (p. 55), both built in Art Nouveau style at the beginning of the 20th century. Here you can enjoy a swim, a Swedish massage, or relax in a sauna, Turkish bath or jacuzzi. Eriksdalsbadet, on the other hand, has even more to offer. Built when Stockholm was bidding for the Olympic Games, it's a huge aquatic centre comprising three pools, gym, solarium, swimming school and restaurant

STOCKHOLM NEW

Launched in 1989 by Claes and Christina Britton, the English language magazine, *Stockholm New*, is published twice a year and features the latest and most avant-garde in Swedish design. Sold in the large hotels in Stockholm and in fashionable outlets and shops, it is a documentary on stylish living with stunning photography and interesting articles. On appropriately glossy paper, it captures what is most hip about Sweden.

(Hammarby slussväg, 20, Metro Skanstull, ☎ 08 508 40 250, open Mon.-Thu. 6.30am-9pm, Fri. 6.30am-8pm, Sat. 9am-5pm, Sun. 9am-6pm).

Centralbadet

The Stockholm Day Spa (p. 97) is also worth a visit. Opened in 2000, under the roof of the huge Åhléns shop, it is the first of its kind in Europe.

Eriksdalsbadet

700 YEARS OF ARCHITECTURE

Since its foundation in the 13th century, Stockholm has undergone a series of transformations. Despite its preservation after the Second World War, part of the city centre was razed in the 1960s in the name of modernism. However, the city has been exceptionally well maintained, and both its traditional and modern aspects continue to live side-by-side in harmony.

A CAPITAL IS BORN

Stockholm first saw the light of day in 1255, when Birger Jarl built a fortress on an island located between Lake Mälaren and the Baltic Sea. The buildings of this period were destroyed by fire in the Middle Ages and all that remains today are the foundations.

THE BAROQUE PERIOD

The Old Town assumed its current form in the 17th and 18th centuries, and according to the plans of Nicodemus Tessin the Older, the royal palace was built in the Italian Baroque style to replace the Three Crowns fortress which

Amongst the various cellars of shops and restaurants, the Storkykobadet is an unusual and fascinating example – a house with two underground levels, boasting a wonderful pool built in a 13th-century vaulted cave lit by candles. The few locals who know about this delight enjoy bathing in the nude here (Svartmagatan, 20, ☎ 08 615 03 00, open Mon. and Thu. 5-8.30pm for women only and Tues. and Fri. 5-8.30pm for men only).

was destroyed by fire. Several palaces and houses were built with pale yellow facades, the simplicity of which contrasted with the opulence of their interiors. In the 18th century, following a trip to France and Italy, King Gustav III commissioned several buildings from his favourite architects and interior decorators, Fredrik Magnus Piper, Olof Tempelman and Louis Masreliez. Among these were the Gustav III Pavilion

(Paviljong) and the beginnings of a royal palace, today preserved in the Haga park. The royal residences in Drottningholm, Ulriksdal and Gripsholm, located outside Stockholm, are magnificent examples of the architecture of this period.

Drottningholm

THE INDUSTRIAL ERA

In the 19th century, industrialisation led to a building boom, which saw the construction of the National

The National Museum

SKOGSKYRKO-GÅRDEN

Built between 1914 and 1940, the cemetery at Skogskyrkogården, listed by UNESCO as a World Heritage Site, is a true haven of peace. Created by Gunnar Asplund and Sigurd Lewerentz, it's the perfect place for a quiet walk after a busy day of sightseeing (Sockenvägen, 492. Enskede. Metro Skogskyrkogården, ☎ 08 508 30 193). Open to the public all year round, there are guided tours on Mondays at 5pm from May to mid-September.

Museum, inspired by the Italian Renaissance, as well as the Opera House, designed in the national academic style. However, it was in the early 20th century that the face of Stockholm changed. The Austrians imported the Viennese Jugendstil, while the Swedes built their Art Nouveau homes, still visible on Strandvägen and along the avenues of Östermalm. It was also the era of the National Romantic movement – the City Hall, built between 1911 and 1923 by Ragna Ostberg, is among the best examples of the style. Swedish architecture enjoyed a golden era in the 1920s. The pure and elegant Swedish Grace style, embodied in the Liljevachs Konsthall designed by Carl Bergsten, still is an inspiration to contemporary architects. The need to provide decent housing for all, however, led to the emergence of Functionalism in the 1930s.

POST WAR

Parts of Stockholm were destroyed in the second half of the 20th century under the banner of modernism. No less than a quarter of the city centre, Klara, was razed to the ground in the 1960s, making room for what is now the City. It was a period of shame for some and of revolution for others, and it was during this time that Peter Celsing built the cultural centre and the Kulturhuset theatre on Sergels Torg. The 1980s were characterised by institutional postmodernism, whereas the 1990s saw the birth of a modernist movement led by Thomas Sandell and Jonas Bohlin. Today, a generation of architects and designers, working in agencies such as Claesson-Koivisto-Rune, and Wö, express themselves in a

The City

very contemporary vein. The library at the Liljevachs Konsthall and the Haga Forum restaurant are excellent illustrations of their style. However, the commission for the new Museum of Modern Art and Architecture, opened in 1998, fell to the Argentinian, Rafael Moneo. Inside, an exhibition narrates the history of Swedish architecture.

Kulturhuset

FOOD, GLORIOUS FOOD

Washed by both the waters of Lake Mälären and the Baltic Sea, Stockholm is the perfect dining venue for lovers of fresh fish and seafood, caught right in the heart of the city. Those who prefer meat won't be disappointed either, as there are plenty of dishes to choose from. The portions are so generous you won't feel remotely hungry after enjoying a meal in one of the many delightful restaurants.

THE *SMÖRGÅSBORD*

The word *smörgås* means 'open sandwich' and *bord* is the Swedish for table. The *smörgåsbord* is very much a symbol of popular cuisine, or *humanskost,* in Sweden. Today it consists of a number of small dishes from which you can take your pick.

the 'Christmas Buffet' and features in all the tourist restaurants and on all the Christmas season menus. Families can often be found enjoying a *smörgåsbord* at Sunday lunchtime in the large restaurants, such as the Veranden in the Grand Hotel (see p. 77).

The tradition dates back to the 18th century when an appetiser buffet was served before the main course at the very best tables in high society. The buffet was composed of savoury dishes washed down with a few shots of schnapps. A lavish version of this is now known as

REGIONAL CUISINE

An authentic *smörgåsbord* can be made up of as many as a hundred different dishes, starting with herring (*sill*), either marinaded, or flavoured in a variety of ways (sweet-pickled, pickled with onions, mustard or dill) and served

with boiled potatoes, cream and chives or dill. To follow, there's marinaded salmon, ox tongue, Swedish onion meatballs served with bilberries, and a variety of salads with a cream or horseradish dressing. Not forgetting the prawns and crayfish and 'Jansson's temptation' (sliced herring, potatoes and onion baked in cream). So you might as well forget the diet!

SIMPLE AND WHOLESOME

Traditional Swedish cooking is characterised by the lack of fresh ingredients in days gone by. Typical rustic recipes include pork, herring, potatoes, beetroot, offal, lard, pâtés, charcuterie and of course fish. The absence of fruit is particularly noticeable, although the odd wild berries do feature, such as bilberries, blackberries, blueberries, blackcurrants and yellow raspberries (which are peculiar to Scandinavia). Dried or smoked reindeer, the basic nourishment for the hunters of the Far North in days of old, has now become a rarity, but you might find it on the shelves of Östermalms Saluhall (see p. 106) at an exorbitant price. In the past, one of the only ways to preserve food was to smoke it, and this tradition is still in vogue today. You can find a delicious range of smoked fish and charcuterie in many of the shops.

BAKERY DELIGHTS

Sweden's pancakes and delicious breads and buns are simply irresistible, particularly when they're served with butter or margarine before a main meal. They come plain or flavoured with cumin seeds, wholegrain or cereal. Large

add a selection of cold delicacies, including salmon, vegetables in mayonnaise and liver pâté (veal or pork).

This is the speciality of the famous Teatergrillen (see p. 81). If you find a cosy little café and are feeling a bit peckish, you should sample some of the

GRAVLAX

Gravlax – dry-cured salmon with salt, sugar and dill – is one of Sweden's best known dishes. Mix four tablespoons of sugar with the same amount of salt and 2 teaspoons of crushed white peppercorns.

Rub mixture over the flesh of two salmon fillets weighing around 500g each and sprinkle with dill. Place one fillet on top of the other, with the flesh of one against the skin of the other. Cover and leave in the refrigerator for 36 hours, turning once. Remove the marinade and slice thinly. Serve with lemon or mustard sauce.

which you'll find just about everywhere; the locals have it with their boiled eggs for breakfast. You may be also surprised to discover other less likely specialities, such as crayfish flavoured cheese spread sold in tubes – worth trying it just for the novelty alone!

COFFEE AND SWEET TREATS

The Swedish may rank second in the world in the per capita coffee-drinking stakes, but their version is generally not ranked quite so highly. It's a rather weak filter coffee that often sits for hours on an electric warmer.

round breads with a hole in the middle are hung on sticks above the counter – an unusual sight if you've never seen them before. The Konsum stores sell a huge range of breads mostly made with organic flour

GASTRONOMIC SPECIALITIES

The Swedes are masters of the sandwich. Using *smörrebröd* (black bread) as a base, they

small, round white bread rolls with cumin, served with sour cream and raw onions. The Swedes are partial to sauces and mayonnaise, and love what they call *bleak roe* (yellow caviar)

However, this is more than made up for by the buns. The traditional *kafferep* (coffee party) includes a minimum of seven different kinds of homemade buns and cakes, including the famous *pepparkakor* or ginger cake. At lunchtime, you'll find most Swedes in a *konditori* with just a coffee and a cinnamon or

revolutionised Swedish gastronomy. A few years ago, Mathias Dahlgren was elected world master chef in Lyons, bringing back the prestigious Bocuse d'Or prize to his home country. Swedish 'nouvelle cuisine' is very different from its French counterpart, and is a successful mix of traditional and borrowed influences. Characterised by its wonderful, fresh ingredients and its large portions, it has a certain 'special something' that adds originality and flavour. New restaurants are opening all the time and the locals are happy to spend the extra krona to enjoy the truly wonderful dishes.

saffron bun.
If you're after a quick energy boost you should try the nation's favourite treat – *Daim* – a crisp toffee bar covered in milk chocolate (known as *Dime*).

A NEW STYLE OF COOKING

At the end of the 1980s a handful of dynamic and innovative young chefs

ALCOHOL – AN EXPENSIVE TREAT

Although they may not like to admit it, the Swedes consume large amounts of alcohol. All the proof you need is available in the crowded bars on Friday and Saturday evenings, when the locals traditionally go out for a drink. This is no doubt due to the very strict laws governing the sale and purchase of alcohol in Sweden. All alcohol (including beer and wine) can only be sold in the state shops, known as System Bolaget, which exercise

a monopoly on alcohol sales. There are no limits on how much you can buy, but the prices are fairly prohibitive due to the high import taxes. The same goes for bars and restaurants, where a bottle of

Alcohol on sale in a System Bolaget store

wine can double the bill. Beer, however, is brewed in Sweden itself and is therefore more affordable.

AQUAVIT AND SCHNAPPS

Aquavit is the principal alcohol produced in Sweden. Made from potatoes, it's a clear liquid with a pungent taste of cumin and aniseed. A strong liqueur, served chilled, it often accompanies the *smörgåsbord*. It's less popular today among the trendy drinkers in Stockholm, but you'll find it on the shelves at System Bolaget. If you want to treat yourself to a bottle, look for the Nils Oscar label.

SKÅL!

To offer a toast in Sweden is more than just a matter of lifting your glass. It's a delicate social exercise. When someone says 'Skål!', those assembled must raise their glass, look each person round the table in the eye, stopping each time to take a sip, and repeat the whole procedure for each of those present. The ceremony can be repeated on a number of occasions during a meal.

Schnapps, on the other hand, comes in several flavours, based on leaves, roots, flowers and berries. With a hundred varieties to choose from, you'll be spoiled for choice. Like aquavit, schnapps is often served with a *smörgåsbord*.

BEER AND VODKA

Since the mid-1980s, beer has become hugely popular in the bars of Stockholm, a cause of great comfort and revenue to Swedish brewers. Legend has it that even the Vikings enjoyed the odd glass of beer, and there is evidence that they had a grain-based drink rather like it. Perhaps that is what gave them their strength and intrepid spirit. In the Middle Ages, the nuns of Solberg convent received a ration of 14 barrels of beer per year, which worked out at around

5 litres per day. It's hard to say if this level of consumption still applies to the folk of Sweden today, but it is unlikely!

There are over a dozen Swedish beers, including Millennium, Norrlands Guild Export and Falcon Export, some of which are exported far beyond the Baltic to other countries. Absolut Vodka is of course very popular in Sweden and is the most widely known brand in the world, thanks to trendy publicity campaigns involving avant-garde designers from all round the world.

WINE

Sweden has no vineyards of its own and therefore has to import all its wine. The Swedes aren't snobbish or prejudiced in their choice of wine and have very experimental palates, enjoying French, Italian, Chilean, South African or Canadian wines. The wine lists at certain restaurants in Stockholm, such as the Operakällaren (see p. 83), are the source of both pleasure and envy for even the best wine connoisseurs.

THE GUSTAVIAN SPIRIT

The Gustavian style is a happy and harmonious mix of the simple and the sophisticated. Its name comes, of course, from King Gustav III, an aesthete and lover of all forms of depictive and decorative art. He had an eye for beautiful objects, inspired perhaps by his French-style education. The very characteristic style of this era can still be found in Swedish palaces today.

Gustav III

that were previously kept closed in the winter months due to the cold were able to remain open throughout the year and became the focus of attention for interior designers and decorators. The most beautiful stoves were those from the Marieberg factory, and as they began to replace fireplaces, they became decorative features in their own right. The tiles were often hand-painted with garlands of flowers, sometimes in several colours.

elements of the Rococo period and the more conservative, classical lines of the 18th century. It was characterised by decorative walls featuring all kinds of

A SIGN OF PROGRESS

The Gustavian style was imposed under the reign of Gustav III, between 1770 and the early 1780s, but it had made an appearance before this period, partly as the result of the invention of a new type of ornate porcelain tile stove in 1767. This creation, combining beauty, efficiency and elegance, was the work of Carl Johan Cronstedt and Fabian Wrede, and made use of an ingenious system of pipes to heat the home more effectively. Some of the rooms

WHERE ROCOCO MEETS CLASSICAL

Gustavian style, unique to Europe, was a combination of the highly imaginative

trompe l'oeil motifs, including garlands of leaves and flowers, marble patterns, medallions and laurel crowns.

Gustav III Paviljong

The designs were painted in very pale and subtle colours on the fabric-covered walls. The true 'Gustavian' colour is a grey-blue, somewhere between azure and faded slate. Even

in those days, light – absent for such long periods during the year – played a vital part in interior decoration. Ceilings were painted white to maximise the effect of light, and were complemented by pale wooden floors and high windows. In aristocratic homes, however, ceilings steadfastly remained painted with *trompe l'oeil* motifs, and it was during this era that the famous *pampille* crystal lights

came into their own. The architecture of the Gustavian period featured houses built on two levels, replacing the three-storey homes of the flamboyant 17th-century. One of the most beautiful examples of this in Stockholm is the Gustav III Paviljong, a small jewel built by the king in the heart of the Haga park (see p. 71). He lived here during the construction of his royal palace, which remained unfinished as he was assassinated before its completion.

(see p. 71)

ONE STYLE SUITS ALL

The Gustavian style was essentially very democratic. Although its motifs were rather refined, the very simplicity of the materials used meant that it was accessible to all – nobility, town dwellers and the less-privileged country folk alike. Since the Renaissance it had been fashionable in high society to retreat to the country during the summer; the rest of the population could also indulge in the same pleasure, albeit in more rustic, but equally charming homes.

FURNITURE

This simple yet elegant Swedish style continues to inspire contemporary designers. However, it was not restricted to just the walls, and was adopted by furniture makers. Chairs from the Gustavian period are a combination of simple lines and classic decoration, such as laurel wreaths – a typical Gustavian chair has an oval back and a seat with rounded edges. The wonderful wooden clocks of this era, painted with floral motifs, are simply a joy to behold.

FABRICS

Simplicity was also the rule in fabric design during this period. In the country, chairs were covered in cotton fabric decorated with stripes or large red or blue checks. In the homes of the nobility, the same patterned material was used to protect the tapestry upholstery on chairs and seats from the harmful rays of the sun. Simple white cotton voile was used to drape around the windows.

ARTS AND CRAFTS – WHERE NATURE MEETS DESIGN

Traditional craftsmen and artisans have always been very influential in the world of Swedish design. Inspired by nature, they source their materials, colours and shapes from the world around them. Swedish design is often functional but also very modern in outlook. The government has long supported it as an industry and it continues to attract new generations of talented designers.

EARTH, AIR AND FIRE

From the end of the 19th century onwards, the two biggest names in Swedish porcelain, Gustavberg and Rörstrand, commissioned out-of-house artists to create new designs for them. These independent ceramic artists soon came up with suitably non-conformist

designs. Asa Lindström, for example, developed the concept of placing photographic images under enamel on his gold-rimmed cups. The art of glass-blowing is also a Swedish speciality. Orrefors and Kosta Boda, both founded in the 18th century, have long been

rivals in this field, but today they form part of the Royal Scandinavian group. Their beautiful glasses with hand-painted tulip motifs are famous throughout the world, as are the popular cat characters designed by Ulrika-Hydman Vallien for Kosta Boda. In more recent times, the Pukeberg company has launched limited edition ranges by young artists.

A CULTIVATED TRADITION

Sweden is justifiably proud of its longstanding arts and crafts association, known as Svenskt Form. Its success came with the Universal Exhibition held in Stockholm in 1897. Industrialisation arrived relatively late in Sweden, but the arts and crafts movement (ceramics, glass, textiles and silverware) was already very strongly rooted in the country. Independent craftsmen come together to form co-operatives in order to share gallery space and sell their work, as well as finding time to work in their studios. The most famous of these galleries is Blås&Knåda, in which 50 glassworkers and ceramic artists display their wonderful pieces (Hornsgatan, 26, Metro Slussen, ☎ 08 642 77 67, open Mon.-Fri. 11am-6pm, Sat. 11am-4pm, Sun. noon-4pm).

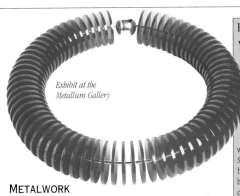

Exhibit at the Metallum Gallery

PIA WALLEN

Working in felt is a long-standing tradition in Sweden, one that has been recognised internationally and given an enormous boost by Pia Wallen. Her creations fall somewhere between fashion and design items and are very simple yet striking, produced in warm, contemporary colours. She is famous not only for her slippers, but also for her bags, cushions and indoor clothing. Keep an eye out for her work on your travels around Stockholm.

METALWORK AND FABRIC DESIGN

The silver- and goldsmiths of today have inherited an ancient tradition, and now experiment combining metal with other materials to make imaginative and innovative creations. Wonderful examples of this can be found in the Metallum Gallery on Hornsgatan in Södermalm (see p. 51) and in the neighbouring galleries of Efva Attling, Smide och Form and Rey Urban (on Sibyllegatan in Östermalm, see p. 111). Textile and fabric design is an equally vibrant field, with natural fibres such as felt, linen or cotton over-printed with naïve, colourful and poetic motifs. The Tiogruppen, now 30 years old, made a very powerful design statement in the 1970s and 1980s with its garish colours, which are now visible in their Götgatan shop in Södermalm. Nina Jobs, part designer, part artisan creates functional designs, sometimes with a double usage.

TRADITION LIVES ON

Contemporary designs never overshadow the traditional arts and crafts, which still flourish in Sweden. Examples can be seen in the open-air museum in Skansen. During the summer, the public can enjoy watching the

glass-blowers, engravers, silversmiths, metalworkers and potters at work, with their creations on sale in the museum's own shop. If you are keen to see more,

head to the island of Fjäderholmarna, about 30 minutes from the city centre, where contemporary artists rent studios during the summer and welcome visitors.

WORKING WITH WOOD

Sweden's famous Dalecarlian wooden horse is a lasting symbol of the very strong tradition of woodworking. It's available in various sizes, hand-painted with floral motifs characteristic of its native region. Wooden kitchen utensils are equally prized and can be seen in the Skansen studios and museum shops. They bear witness to the continuing vitality of the tradition and stand alongside the famous Swedish clogs made today in the trendiest of colours, ranging from shocking pink to vibrant apple green.

MODERN ART

The inhabitants of Stockholm claim that their city is home to the largest number of exhibition spaces in Europe. Well, it's certainly true that art is on view almost everywhere in Stockholm – in the museums, art galleries, craft studios and even in the metro, two thirds of which features the work of contemporary artists. Art is universally accessible in Sweden, thanks to significant support from the state.

AN UNDERGROUND GALLERY

Try to imagine the largest and longest art gallery in the world (110km/59 miles), dug deep below the earth's surface and used every day by hundreds of thousands of people. The Stockholm metro is just that, and it's a source of national pride for the Swedes. Since the late 1940s, when the first metro line was completed, the local council has commissioned artists and craftsmen to transform the stations into areas of popular culture. Travelling on the metro is certainly an eye-catching experience, and in the last 40 years, no fewer

than 130 artists have made their mark on a total of 70 of the 100 stations. Today, the body in charge of this work has an annual budget of 2.5 million krona, allowing you to see statues, paintings, engravings, mosaics, ceramics, maps and sculptures at every turn. Rinkeby station resembles a cave, with its mosaics portraying scenes from the Viking era. At the

Tegnergatan exit (towards the Strindberg Museum) to Rådmansgatan station, you can see an enamel depiction of Strindberg himself, the most famous Swedish author and landscape painter, who did not win recognition until after his death.

A MOVE AGAINST ACADEMICISM

From the end of the 19th century, modern Swedish artists reacted against the teaching of the strict academic style that prevailed in the world of fine arts at that time. Whether classical or modern in their approach, artists were equally moved by their own country. They depicted the permanent duality existing between the inspiration of nature and the influence of an industrialised society with the same fervour. At the turn of the 20th century, the voices of those opposed to academicism could be heard loud and clear in their refusal to submit to academic authority.

They turned towards other countries while proposing reforms on the status of indigenous artists. Some of these rebels, such as Karl Nordström, Nils Krueger and Carl Larsson, established themselves on the outskirts of Paris, in Grès-sur-Loing.

Milles is almost equally famous outside Sweden, and international institutions have commissioned many of his works, replicas of which can be admired in his outdoor museum, Millesgården (see box), on the island of Lidingö, northeast of the city centre.

FROZEN IN TIME

On the island of Lidingö stands the magnificent home of the sculptor and art collector, Carl Milles. You can admire his collection and his studio, and take a walk in the gardens among his outdoor sculptures, which look as if they are hanging in the air, suspended in space and time. The view from the terraced promontory is remarkable. To reach the stunning Millesgården (Carl Milles Väg, 2, ☎ 08 446 75 90) take the metro to Ropsten and then any of the following buses: 201, 202, 204, 207, or 212. It's open every day 10am-5pm (15 May to 31 Aug.) and Tue.-Fri. noon-4pm, Sat., Sun. 11am-5pm (1 Sept. to 14 May).

Getting Ready for a Game, *Carl Larsson, 1901*

Without a doubt, the key figures of this movement were Carl Larsson (known for his middle class, domestic interiors), Siri Derkert (one of the few women painters), Axel Nilsson and Ivan Aguéli. Art from between the 19th and early 20th century is well represented in the National Art Museum (see p. 61), the private collections of Prince Eugene, housed in the Waldemarsudde estate (see p. 66), and in the Thielska Gallery (see p. 66).

SCULPTURE

Two great sculptors, with radically different styles, dominated the field at the beginning of the 20th century: Carl Eldh and Carl Milles. Eldh's work can be seen on the steps of the town hall by the shores of Lake Mälaren, whereas Milles' creations are dotted around the whole city.

A SENSE OF PATRONAGE

Today, contemporary art benefits both from the support of institutions and of private foundations. The new Museum of Modern Art (see p. 60) organises exhibitions of the work of young, contemporary artists, and also finances new and emerging talent on an annual basis. Even the well-known vodka brand, Absolut, has an impressive private collection of contemporary art, and commissions artists to

create pieces that interpret its now famously shaped bottle. Photographs of this work are regularly published in magazines and are often used in publicity material.

MUSIC AND FILM

Swedish film has reached almost mystical status outside its own country, thanks to the huge success of its stars. The music industry received a major boost in the 1970s, with the meteoric rise to international fame of Abba, whose songs have become popular classics throughout the world. Swedish pop groups and bands continue to sing in English and sales are still going strong.

SWEDISH STARS

Strangely enough, Swedish cinema is best represented outside its own country, where its stars have received international acclaim. This process began in the 1920s, during the era of silent films, when Greta Garbo left for Hollywood and starred in such unforgettable films as *Anna Karenina* and *Grand Hotel*. Still in Hollywood in the 1950s, Ingrid Bergman captured the hearts of such

stars as Humphrey Bogart, Gary Cooper and Gregory Peck as the beautiful, cool, distant, elegant Nordic woman in such timeless classic as *Casablanca, Anastasia* and *Gaslight*. And who could possibly forget the voluptuous Anita Ekberg bathing in Rome's spectacular Trevi fountain in *La Dolce Vita*? Ingmar Bergman, Sweden's best known film director and screenwriter, discovered the esteemed Swedish actor, Max von Sydow, who debuted in Bergman's acclaimed *The Seventh Seal* before going on to star in *The Greatest Story Ever Told*.

Ingrid Bergman

THE MAN HIMSELF – INGMAR BERGMAN

Bergman has been Sweden's best-known film director since the mid-1960s and is still considered to be the father of contemporary Swedish film, although today he lives hidden away on the island of Fårö. Three-time Oscar winner, he is famed for a prolific output of film classics including *Fanny and Alexander*, *Wild Strawberries* and *The Seventh Seal*, as well as for his theatrical career, which saw him appointed to the post of director of Stockholm's royal theatre.

Greta Garbo's grave

POP MUSIC

What do the following bands have in common: Roxette, Ace of Base, The Cardigans, Europe, Army of Lovers, The Wannadies, The Hives and Abba? All these pop, rock and hard-rock groups are not only internationally famous but, you may be surprised to discover, are also Swedish. The huge success enjoyed by Abba, following their Eurovision Song Contest win in 1974 with the unforgettable *Waterloo*, was not just a one-off. There is a lot happening on the Swedish music scene today, with Swedish groups and bands continuing to make their mark on the international charts.

FROM THE CRADLE TO THE GRAVE

From a very early age Swedish children are taught to play an instrument at the communal music school, which was established after the war and is still an integral part of the Swedish education system. A large number of adults also play instruments in ad hoc groups or sing in choirs, so you may come across a rehearsal in one of the local churches.

THE INFLUENCE OF THE BEATLES

The birth of Swedish pop music came after the Beatles toured the country in 1963. Just a few weeks after they left, around a hundred groups appeared on the music scene, including the rock group The Spotnicks, originally from Gothenburg, who made it into the English charts before touring Europe, the US and Japan. Other groups went on to achieve great success in the wake of Abba, and still

continue to strut their stuff in the English language.

AN IMPORTANT INDUSTRY

Due to the intense activity and success of its pop and rock bands, Sweden ranks third in the CD export charts, hot on the heels of the US and the UK. Music such a flourishing industry that the government created an award in 1997 for the highest number of CDs exported from Sweden. The first winners of this prestigious prize were The Cardigans, having sold 4 million albums worldwide, and new bands such as The Hives are following closely in their footsteps. However, the price of CDs here is about the same as in the rest of Europe, so don't expect any special deals!

ABBA – A LEGEND

There can't be many people who haven't heard the song *Dancing Queen* by Abba. Their kitschy pop songs don't embarrass Swedes in any way – in fact they're immensely proud of the group and their amazing stage outfits, not least because they sold around 200 million records worldwide. The Nordic Museum even devoted an exhibition to the group in 2000, which lasted almost two years. The myth remains intact, even though the couples have now separated.

What to see practicalities

GETTING AROUND

For a capital city, Stockholm is easy to find your way around. You can get almost anywhere on foot (see map at front of guide), and it only takes about half an hour to walk across the centre of the city (west to east or north to south). The public transport system (SL or *Storstockholms Lokaltrafik*) also operates efficiently and the metro system (*Tunnelbana/ T-bana*), comprising three main lines (see map at back of guide), covers a large part of the city (over a total of 110 km/70 miles). The metro stations are something of a cultural experience, filled with contemporary paintings and sculptures, but it's not always obvious which platform or line to take.

Some stations have a number of exits (marked with a T-sign) which can be at a considerable distance from each other, so if you choose the wrong exit, you could end up having to walk quite a way. However, if you want to give your feet a rest during your break, the most pleasant and eco-friendly way to travel is by bus. In an effort to cut pollution, the buses run on ethanol (produced partly from Spanish red wine!), and their routes are clearly marked on the official bus maps that you can buy from tourist offices (40kr). A single ticket costs around 16kr and is valid for two hours travel anywhere on the bus system. For 110kr you can buy *rabattkuponger* (coupons) that allow you to make 20 reduced-price trips. On each journey you must show your coupon to the

driver (bus) or controller (metro) and they will check or stamp it for you. Tickets can be purchased in the metro stations or tobacconists (*Pressbyro*), but not on the bus itself. Swedes are very family oriented and allow children to travel free of charge on public transport, as well as pregnant women and parents travelling with children in pushchairs or prams. The bus platforms are at pavement height, which makes it easy to board the bus. Seats at the front are for people with allergies, so in the unlikely event you are travelling with a dog, choose a seat at the back!

BY TAXI

There are three official taxi companies in the capital:

Taxi Stockholm:
☎ 08 15 00 00

CIVIC PRIDE

Swedes have a firmly rooted sense of civic pride. They respect both their environment (never discarding litter in the streets) and the highway code. Motorists never jump traffic lights and religiously abide by the rules at pedestrian crossings and cycle lanes. Even the pedestrians wait patiently at the side of the road until it's their turn to cross. At major road junctions, traffic signals are both visual and audible, regulated by a beeping tone (a fast tone for pedestrians and slower one for motorists) to help blind people to cross the road. In public places, such as museums and shops, you'll always find a ramp for wheelchair users and pushchairs.

Taxi Kurir: ☎ 08 30 00 00

Topcab: ☎ 08 33 33 33

All of these operators charge the same fixed prices, clearly shown on the meter, and will automatically give you a receipt. The other taxis you will see (also black), are operated by independent firms or individuals, and prices tend to fluctuate, sometimes dramatically. You're better off choosing one of the official firms – look out for their names on the side of the vehicles. You can hail a taxi in the street or go to a taxi rank. When you phone for a taxi, wait for the recorded message (in Swedish only) to finish and then speak to the operator, who will take your address and destination, and

give you the car number and your reservation number. If this sounds too daunting, you can always ask the hotel or restaurant to book for you. A trip across the city centre will cost around 100-200kr.

BY BIKE

Bike rental is not particularly cheap, but it is a wonderful way to travel in the summer months, and there's a system of cycle paths, respected by cars and mopeds (there are only a few of the latter, anyway). Whenever they can, Stockholmers leave their cars at home and head off on two wheels. It's more enjoyable and more environmentally friendly. The crime level is almost non existent, so there's no need to worry about having your bike stolen, even if you leave it somewhere for a whole day. You can hire bikes for around 250kr per day from **Djurgårdsbrons Sjöcafé**, at the entrance to Djurgården, on the left after the bridge (☎ 08 660 57 57, open end April-end Sept. every day 9am-9pm).

BY BOAT

It's certainly worth taking a trip around the city centre by ferry. The one at Djurgården makes a number of stops on the island (including Skansen and Gröna Lund) and also goes to the island of Skeppsholmen. It operates all year round from Skeppsbron, but in the summer months, it also goes from Nybroplan. For more information ☎ 08 679 58 30. The ferry is part of the urban transport system and tickets and vouchers are therefore valid for travel.

THE STOCKHOLM CARD

Buying a *Stockholmskortet* is an excellent idea. It gives you unlimited travel on city buses, ferries, metro and regional trains, as well as free entry to around 70 museums, free parking in the town centre, a guided boat tour of the city (in summer only) and a pocket guide. All this for just 199kr (24 hours), 398kr (48 hours) or 498kr (72 hours). Children aged between 7 and 17 are charged 35kr for 24 hours. You can buy it from any tourist office, at the Hotellcentralen in the main hall of the Central Station and in the metro stations.

GUIDED TOURS

A good way to get to know the basic layout of the city is with a guided tour, accompanied by a local expert. The **Stockholm Information Service** at the main tourist office (☎ 08 789 24 90/96, 🖶 08 789 25 10, email: guides@stinfo.se, website: www.stoinfo.se) will find you a suitable guide and can arrange a tour of the archipelago. Alternatively, a taxi guide can take you around the city, but remember to agree the price when booking, or with the driver when you get in. Phone the main tourist office (on the above number), or call directly on ☎ 08 612 00 00. If you fancy a trip around the archipelago, then try one of the packages at the *Utflyksbutiken*, also in the main tourist office on the ground floor of *Sverigehuset* (Sweden House), on

Hamngatan in Norrmalm (☎ 08 789 24 00), or check out the options on-line at www.stockholmtown.com. Several companies also offer panoramic bus tours with a variety of different routes. **City Sightseeing Tours** (☎ 08 587 140 30, email: sightseeing@stromma.se) leave from the Opera (or from your hotel if you prefer and at no extra charge), and their tours last an hour and

a half or three hours. If you are feeling more romantic, try one of their carriage tours or a dinner cruise in the archipelago (summer only). **Stockholm Sightseeing** (☎ 08 587 140 20) also operates similar tours, which depart from the Grand Hotel.

USING THE TELEPHONE

To call Sweden from abroad, dial the international access code followed by 46 for Sweden, then dial the area code (omitting the first 0 – so dial 8 for Stockholm) and the number. To call abroad from Sweden, dial 00 followed by the required country code:

UK: ☎ 44
Republic of Ireland: ☎ 353
USA: ☎ 1
Australia: ☎ 61
Canada: ☎ 1
New Zealand: ☎ 64

If you're phoning from a hotel, dial 0 to get an outside line. You'll find it much cheaper to use the public payphones, all of which take cards and can be found in even the tiniest villages. You can call anywhere in the world from a public booth using a phonecard (sold at newsagents or Pressbyro tobacconists in units of 30, 60 and 120) or your credit card. Instructions are generally displayed inside the booth. A call within Europe will cost around 6kr per minute. Of course, you can use your mobile phone if you have international access, but

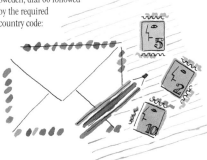

check the overseas rate before you leave. It's also worth knowing that information lines, which often begin with 020, are tollfree within Sweden, but cannot be called from outside the country.

WRITING HOME

Post offices are open Mon.-Fri. 9.30am-6pm and Sat. 10am-1pm. You can buy stamps (*frimärken*), postcards (*vykort*) and all the stationery you need to keep in touch with friends and family. Don't just get into the queue – take a number when you arrive and wait for your turn. Sending a letter (up to 20g) or postcard within Europe costs 7kr – anything heavy is weighed and priced accordingly. It should take around 2 days to reach a European destination. You can also buy stamps in newspaper kiosks and tobacconists (*Pressbyro*) – you may even find your hotel sells them. The main post office in the Central Station is open Mon.-Fri. 7am-10pm, Sat. and Sun. 10am-7pm.

INTERNET CAFÉS

The most user-friendly internet café is in the basement of the Kulturhuset, Sergels Torg, 3, ☎ 08 508 31 489, open Mon.-Fri. 10am-7pm, Sat., Sun. 11am-5pm.

INTERNATIONAL NEWSPAPERS

If you can't live without your paper, head for the Press Stop shops, where the choice is endless. You'll find outlets at Götgatan, 31, Kungsgatan, 14, Sveävagen, 52 and Drottninggatan, 35.

CHANGING MONEY

Banks are open Mon.-Fri. 10am-3pm (Thu. to 5.30pm), but closed at weekends and public holidays. The SEB at Arlanda airport, however, is open every day 6.30am-9pm. You can also change money at the bureaux de change (but check the commission first). You'll find these on the ground floor of the huge NK store, Sverigehuset, Central Station, the main tourist office and at a number of other addresses, including Vasagatan, 14, Sveavägen, 14, Kungsgatan, 2 and Götgatan, 94

TOURIST OFFICES

The main tourist office is in Sverigehuset (Sweden House) at Hamngatan, 27 (on corner of Kungsträdgården, open Mon.-Fri. 8am-7pm, Sat.-Sun. 9am-5pm, ☎ 08 789 24 00). It's a mine of information and

should have the answers to all your questions. You can arrange and pay for excursions, make hotel reservations and buy tickets for shows. On the second floor is the Swedish Institute's library, where you'll find a vast array of history books, collections of recipes and general information about the city in a number of languages.

MUSEUMS

Museums are open Tues.-Sun., closing late (8pm) on Tues. You can safely leave your coats and baggage locked away, free of charge, in their automatic cloakrooms (you'll need a 5kr coin, which you'll get back). Most museums supply free pushchairs, wheelchairs and portable folding seats for those who have difficulty standing for long periods.

Gamla Stan, three adjoining islands

In 1255, Birger Jarl erected a fortification on three adjoining pieces of land, and it was this event that initiated the creation of Stockholm. Little remains of the original medieval structures, but despite the invasion of tourist shops, Gamla Stan retains almost all of its ancient, historic charm. It gets particularly busy at the weekend, but its narrow streets are easy to explore on foot or by bike, and are definitely worth visiting.

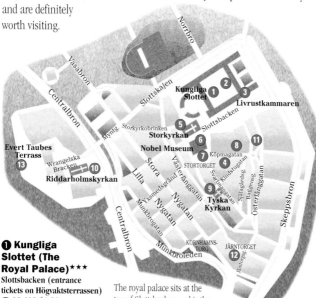

❶ Kungliga Slottet (The Royal Palace)★★★

Slottsbacken (entrance tickets on Högvaktsterrassen)
☎ 08 402 61 30
Open Tue.-Sun. noon-3pm (1 Sept.-14 May), every day 10am-4pm (14 May-31 Aug.).
Entrance charge.

The royal palace sits at the top of Slottsbacken and is the official residence of Sweden's royal family, although they actually live in the royal palace at Drottningholm. Built in the 18th century by Tessin the Younger, it rivals Versailles or Buckingham Palace in its magnificence, not only for the number of rooms (over 600), but also for its stunning interiors and interesting treasures. You can visit the Throne Room and the huge and sumptuous apartments with their wonderful collection of furniture and tapestries. (See also p. 132.)

❷ The Treasury★★

Slottsbacken
☎ 08 402 61 30
Open Tue.-Sun. noon-3pm (1 Sept.-14 May), every day 10am-4pm (14 May-31 Aug.).
Entrance charge.

Sheltered in the medieval foundations of the original palace lies the Treasury with

THE CHANGING OF THE GUARD★★

If you love pageantry and royal folklore, don't miss this ceremony, which takes place in entrance court of the palace to a musical accompaniment. It lasts almost an hour and involves regiments from all over Sweden. Make sure you arrive in plenty of time (Apr.-Oct. Wed. and Sat. 12.15pm, Sun. and public hols 1.15pm. June-Aug. Mon.-Sat. 12.15pm, Sun. and public hols 1.15pm).

its wonderful array of royal jewels, the most ancient of which, King Gustav Vasa's sword, dates from the 15th century. There are jewel-studded crowns, sceptres and town keys, as well as delicate jewellery and finery, which will capture the imagination and transport you back to another age.

❸ Livrust-kammaren (The Royal Armoury)★★

Slottsbacken
☎ 08 519 555 44
Open Tue.-Sun. 11am-5pm (Thurs. to 8pm) (Sept.-May), every day 10am-5pm (June-Aug.).
Entrance charge.

This award-winning museum is also hidden in the vaults. The Royal Armoury, which is more about ceremony than weapons, is home to some stunning pieces, including suits of armour, costumes and

carriages dating back as far as the 16th century. Gold brocade, obviously the fashion at royal weddings, coronations and official ceremonies, is much in evidence. Among the more extraordinary items are the official sleighs that made their way through the town's snow-covered cobbled streets.

❹ Grillska Konditoriet★★

Stortorget, 3
☎ 08 787 86 05
Open Mon.-Fri. 9am-6pm, Sat.-Sun. 11am-6pm.

This is the place to come for breakfast, a light lunch or

Sunday brunch. Welcoming and atmospheric, it combines a subtle mix of the new and the old. You can choose a daily special (soup, quiche or salad), followed by one of the tempting pastries on offer, before settling down to eat in one of the three dining rooms. The red and sky-blue walls are covered with attractive, modern paintings, and on sunny days, you can sit on the terrace and listen to a concert.

❺ Storkyrkan (Great Church)★★★

Trångsund, 1
☎ 08 723 30 21
Open every day 9am-4pm (9am-6pm 14 May-15 Sept.).
Free entrance.
Guided tours available 1 July-19 Aug (fee charged).

The highest point of the old part of Stockholm is crowned by Storkyrkan, the city's cathedral, built on the site of a church constructed by Birger Jarl in the 13th century. Renovated in the 15th century, it was then sumptuously remodelled in Baroque style two centuries later. Don't miss the stunning black and silver altarpiece, the royal pews and the 15th-century statue of St George and the Dragon, a replica of which stands in Köpmantorget Square at the end of Bollhusgränd Street. There's also an amazing 16th-century painting of a parhelion, a phenomenon seen in the skies above Stockholm in April 1535 when six halos appeared, looking like false suns. It gives a great idea of what the city looked like at the time. (See also p. 131.)

❻ Nobel Museum★
Stockholm Stock Exchange, Stortorget
☎ 08 23 25 06
Open every day 10am-6pm, Tue. 10am-8pm (May-Aug.); Tue. 11am-8pm, Wed.-Sun. 11am-5pm (Sept.-Apr.); closed public hols. Entrance charge.

The former Stock Exchange now houses the Nobel Museum, opened in April 2001 to mark the centenary of the prize. It's a modern affair, with portraits of the prize winners suspended in the entrance hall. The rooms display information on the winners, their inventions or creations, and even some of their personal effects. You can listen to recordings of their acceptance speeches and fill in any gaps on the interactive site. There are guided tours in English at 11am and 4pm (no extra charge).

❼ Stortorget★★
Gamla Stan's main square, with its tall, narrow, ochre-coloured or red facades, bears witness to the German presence in the past, when the Hanseatic trade flourished (from the 16th century onwards). Stortorget was an execution site during the 'Stockholm Blood Bath' of 1520, when 80 Swedish noblemen were executed and their bodies burned by invading Danish soldiers trying to take the city. Today, it's a perfect place to go for a walk and meet friends. It's also home to the Christmas markets and, in the spring, is filled with the sounds of musical groups and orchestras.

❽ Ljunggrens★
Köpmangatan, 3
☎ 08 676 03 83
Open Tue.-Fri. 11am-6pm, Sat. 11am-3pm, closed Sat. in July.

This lovely old-fashioned shop sells paper in all sizes, shapes, textures and colours, as well as scented inks and sets of coloured wax and stamps with which to personalise your stationery. There are also some lovely cards and photo albums on sale, which have been handcrafted in the studio.

❾ Tyska Kyrkan (German Church)★★★
Tyska Brinken
Open Sat.-Sun. noon-4pm.

This unusual church is an architectural gem that houses

a number of treasures. From the 16th century, Stockholm's important German community were allowed to bring in their own priests to lead their congregations with complete autonomy, and this chapel, built around 1607, was home to the first German parish abroad. In the 17th century the Baroque decorators gave it a sumptuous new interior, with a stunning altarpiece, pulpit and royal pews.

❿ Riddarholms-kyrkan★★
Riddarholmen
Open every day 10am-4pm (15 May-31 Aug.), Sat.-Sun. noon-3pm (Sept.); closed Oct.-Apr.

Cross the Gamla Stan bridge onto Riddarholmen (Island of the Nobles) proper, and you'll find the Riddarholmskyrkan, originally a Franciscan monastery, built and modified between the 13th and 19th centuries. It has been the burial place of Swedish royalty for over six centuries and houses the tombs of Karl XII, Gustav III and Karl Johan XIV, among others. There's a lovely sense of serenity in the place, particularly when it's bathed in soft sunlight, and if you're fortunate, you may even get to hear a rehearsal of religious chants on your visit.

⓫ Knits★★
Österlånggatan, 12
☎ **08 21 08 55**
Open Mon.-Fri. 11am-6pm, Sat. 11am-4pm.

Inger Oddmark Dahlin owns this pretty shop with a vaulted roof that sells woollen items in a variety of styles and colours. His mission is to showcase the talent of young creative Scandinavians, as well as that of Scottish, Italian and Peruvian designers. He sells beautiful jumpers and some very original creations, but they can be quite pricey.

⓬ Järntorget★
Järntorget lies at the intersection of two main axes – Österlånggatan and Västerlånggatan – and is the perfect spot to take a break in one of the tearooms (*konditori*) that surround it. They can be a little touristy, but are still very charming. In summer, groups of masseurs gather on the square offering Swedish massages to passers-by. No need to take any clothes off – just sit down and relax for a few minutes and enjoy being pampered.

⓭ Evert Taubes Terrass★★
Situated to the west of Riddarholmen island, and bereft of shops, bars, restaurants (and therefore tourists), Evert Taubes Terrass looks out over Lake Mälaren. From the outset, this district attracted people who wanted to enjoy the sunshine and the magnificent view over the western area of the city.

Söder, around the Vita Bergen hill

Södermalm – known simply as 'Söder' – was once an isolated working-class suburb. Today, however, it's home to a trendy and arty crowd and is almost a separate town in itself. Distinct from the city centre, it has its own collection of shops, bars, restaurants and beautiful, green areas where you can sit and relax. There are plenty of interesting places to visit and the traditional wooden cottages, which still exist in some parts, contribute to its special character.

Katarinahissen ❶

Klevgränd ❷ Stadsgårdsleden
❺ Katarinavägen
Södra Teatern
Götgatan Östgötag. Högbergsgatan
Nytorgsgatan
Renstiernas Gata
Borgmästargatan
Folkkungagatan
Folkungagatan
❶❷ Tjärhovsgatan Erstagatan Åsögatan
MEDBORGARPLATSEN Folkkungagatan
Kocksgatan ❾ Södermannagatan Bondegatan
❻ Åsögatan Skånegatan
Götgatan Bondegatan ❿ **Sofia Kyrka** **Spårvägsmuseet** ❸
❽ ❼ ❹
Vita Bergen
Barnängsgatan Tegelviksgatan
Katarina Malmgårdsvägen
Bangata

❶ Katarina-hissen★★★

Open Mon.-Sat. 7.30am-10pm, Sun. 10am-10pm. Entrance charge.

At the horrendously busy traffic interchange at Slussen, that links Södermalm to the rest of the city, stands a metal observation tower. Inside a lift

will take you up to the terrace of the Gondolen restaurant, from where the view over the old town and the waterfront is quite amazing. After taking a few obligatory photographs, you can follow the wooden passage that crosses Katarinavägen and leads to Mosebacketorg square, which is particularly pretty with old-fashioned charm.

❷ Södra Teatern★★★

Mosebacke Torg, 3
☎ **08 556 972 30**
Terrace: open every day 11am-1am.

Since the 19th century, this unusual spot has served not only as Söder's theatre and

cultural centre, but as a café by day and a popular bar and disco by night. Some of Sweden's greatest 20th-century artists have performed here, and their signed portraits hang on the walls of the restaurant. The view from the terrace garden over Djurgården and Skeppsholmen, inspired August Strindberg to write the opening pages of his novel *The Red Room*. To commemorate this historic work, a sculpture of the great man appears on the terrace, his eyes gazing towards the horizon. It's a great spot to meet friends and enjoy a drink in the summer.

BOHEMIAN PARADISE

Söder used to be very much a working-class area but over the course of the last 20 years, it has gradually become Stockholm's most bohemian spot. It is just as difficult, and expensive, to find a place to rent here as in the city centre. Home to actors, designers, artists and the avant-garde, it's the perfect setting for Greta Garbo Square.

❸ Spårvägsmuseet (Transport Museum)★
Tegelviksgatan, 22
☎ 08 559 031 80
Open Mon.-Fri. 10am-5pm, Sat.-Sun. 11am-4pm.

This small museum, situated near the Söderhallen coach station, covers more than 100 years of the history of public transport, from horse-drawn carriages to the most recent metro trains. With over 60 vehicles on display, here you can see Stockholm's old tramcars and its very first buses, as well as learn about the city's waterways, which have always been used to move people and cargo. The history of the metro – an underground museum in itself, featuring the work of contemporary artists – is also narrated.

❹ Vita Bergen hill
The area around the church of St Sofia, seemingly forgotten by time, is very attractive, with its little allotment gardens separated by bright red fences.

The tool sheds don't look as if they've been altered since they were built in the 19th century. Fortunately it's now a protected site. To the south, Eriksdalslunden park is home to similar gardens around Arstaviken bay, one of the bends in Lake Mälaren.

❺ Ten Swedish Designers★★★
Götgatan, 25
☎ 08 643 25 04
Open Mon.-Fri. 11am-6pm, Sat. 11am-4pm.

This group is made up of textile designers (including

Gunila Axen, Britt-Marie Christofferson, Carl-Johan de Geer and Inez Svensson), whose creations are colourful and quirky. To celebrate 30 years of activity, the National Museum put on a

(the owner of the gallery) is one of the most well-known in Sweden and includes the designs of Björn Dahlström. His comfy chairs, complete with sleeping bag and his foam rubber seats

wonderful exhibition of their work. Make sure you visit their shop just to see their range of beautiful fabrics, which you can buy by the metre or made up into a variety of delightful items. The handbags, purses and aprons are particularly attractive.

❻ Klara★★★
Nytorgsgatan, 36
☎ 08 694 92 40
Open Mon.-Fri. 11am-6pm, Sat. 11am-4pm.

Here you can get a real feel for the creative spirit at work in contemporary Swedish design. Founded in 1980 by Stefan Ytterborn, the CBI label

shaped like boats are well worth a closer look. There's also a fabulous canopy bed designed by James Irvine. Beauty and style do not come cheap, however, and you may find the table accessories and smaller items more within your budget.

❼ Star People Design★
Katarina Bangata, 17
☎ 08 640 88 95
Open Mon.-Fri. 11am-6pm, Sat. 11am-4pm.

All the items on display in this hippy, laid-back shop are imported from London, from where the owner originally hails. You'll find Indian clothes, skimpy T-shirts with all sorts of logos and designs, gadgets of every kind that would appeal to a younger sibling, striking jewellery and a whole host of other temptations. It's a real Aladdin's cave,

with a selection of incense sticks and books on alternative philosophy.

❽ Kryskolla★
Katarina Bangata, 13
☎ 08 642 91 06
Open Mon. noon-6pm, Tue.-Fri. 11am-6pm, Sat. noon-4pm.

This temple of kitsch may come as a bit of a surprise. Everything on sale has a religious theme of some kind – there are illuminated statues of the Virgin Mary from Lourdes, terracotta angels

and cherubs, plastic Buddhas in a delicate shade of baby pink, fountains and Christ figures that can wink. Ulla Norberg is a New Age high priestess, Feng Shui devotee and owner of the shop.

9 Café String★★★
Nytorgsgatan, 38
☎ 08 714 85 14
Open Mon.-Fri. 9.30am-9pm, Sat.-Sun. 10.30am-9pm.

Beware – Café String is a resolutely trendy spot. The food isn't fabulous, but the cakes and snacks are fine and even quite moderately priced. It's the sort of place people come for a drink, a bite to eat and to see and be seen, and what's more, if you really like it you can even buy the furniture. Oddly enough, everything here is for sale – the furniture, the decorations and even the crockery.

11 Nina Jobs★★★
Nytorgsgatan, 11a
☎ 08 650 05 23.

Nina, a talented graphic artist and designer, prints her own fabrics and models them into

10 Lounge 51 and WC Bar★★★
Skånegatan, 51
☎ 08 641 90 82
Open noon-1am (Sept.-May), 5pm-1am (June-Aug.).

There are two reasons to head for this unusually named venue: it has a restaurant serving unpretentious, international cuisine and a welcoming, unfeasibly long bar. The interior has an interesting decor of recycled items, including a toilet bowl draped in plants (hence the name), positioned at the entrance to the bar. It's a great spot to come to meet friends and enjoy a cocktail standing at the long bar.

functional everyday items with attractive, contemporary shapes and colours. Her floor cushion with handles can also be used as a linen basket, whilst her fabric plant pot transforms itself into a storage container. You do need an appointment to visit her

office/showroom, but her simple yet creative designs are certainly worth a closer look. All her products carry her signature label in the form of a star motif.

12 Medborgar-platsen★
This square is reminiscent of Hötorget, the cobbled square in the city centre. They both share a few things in common: covered markets (*Söderhallarna*), a fruit and vegetable market, cinemas, a shopping centre and a library. What's unique to Medborgarplatsen, however, is its collection of tattoo parlours and body-piercing shops. You can therefore understand why it's a popular meeting place for local youngsters and students.

Södermalm, from Slussen to Långholmen

Hornsgatan stretches from Slussen to the bridge over to the island of Liljeholmen. It's one of Söder's liveliest streets and home to the Folk Operan. Each area has its own character – art galleries to the north, clothes shops to the south – and in the middle lies the statue of the Viking god Thor. To the west is Långholmen, an island once famous for its prisons, dating to the 18th century. All that remains today is the royal jail, which forms part of a prison museum.

❶ Stadsmuseet (City Museum)★

Ryssgården, Slussen
☎ 08 508 316 00
Open Tue.-Sun. 11am-5pm, Thurs. 11am-7pm.

This 17th-century building houses a record of Stockholm's architectural past and the way of life of its inhabitants from the 17th-to 20th centuries. The history of the city as a seaport and industrial centre is retold with models and reconstructed scenes from the daily life of Stockholm folk. The collection includes a 13th-century tavern, a 19th-century classroom, artisan studios from the early 20th century

and a display of domestic comforts from the 1950s.

❷ Jonas Bohlin★★★

Sodermalmstorg, 4
☎ 08 615 23 89
Open Tue. & Thur. noon-6pm.

One of Sweden's most famous designer architects (who ranks alongside his colleague Thomas Sandell in importance), established this gallery in 2000, where he exhibits his furniture, lights and other objects. One of the highlights of the collection is his celebrated lamp in the shape of a fluorescent green tutu, which can be seen in the dining room of the Sturehof restaurant and in one of the rooms of the Birger Jarl hotel.

❸ Söder Mälarstand★★★

If you fancy a romantic walk along a path overlooking the

northern coast of Södermalm, then make your way along Söder Mälarstrand and enjoy the views over the city as you wander past the rows of red

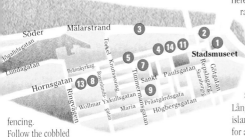

fencing.

Follow the cobbled streets lined with lovely old houses (Bellmansgatan, Bastugatan, Tavastgatan, Brännkyrkagatan, Blecktorns-gränd) before treating yourself to some refreshment in the Mariahissen café (open 9am-4pm) at the end of Bellmansgatan. From here the view over Lake Mälaren and Gamla Stan is really quite something.

❹ The Tea Centre of Stockholm★
Hornsgatan, 46
☎ 08 640 42 10
Open Mon.-Fri. 9.30am-6pm, Sat. 10am-2pm.

This is the place to come if you have had your fill of

Swedish coffee. The owner is Indian and he imports all his tea from Asia, blending his own mixtures. He's happy to spend time discussing his favourite subject with you

whilst you enjoy a refreshing cuppa, and you can sample a selection of biscuits, jams or perfumed honey, all made using tea.

❺ Olivstycket★★
Hornsgatan, 66
☎ 08 658 47 91
Open Mon.-Fri. 11am-6pm, Sat. 11am-3pm.

If you prefer shopping with a conscience – this is the place to come. Known as 'The Corset', this fabric workshop is run by a collective of women in exile in Stockholm. Here they make and sell a range of tasteful, modern clothes, bags, trays and lengths of fabric printed with attractive, humorous motifs.

❻ Långholmen Strandbad★
Långholmen (meaning 'long island') is a delightful place for a walk. The last remaining prison on the island has been turned into a hotel, youth hostel and small museum. There's a tiny beach with rocks, which is popular with swimmers and sunbathers, but if you don't fancy getting wet, you can just wander along the streets and admire the pretty houses and quaint kitchen gardens.

❼ Magritte★

Hornsgatan, 29d
☎ 08 702 94 90
Open Mon.-Fri. 11am-6.30pm, Sat. 11am-3pm.

In her shop Annbritt Enochsson showcases the creations of some talented young Swedish and Scandinavian designers. Her range is both extremely trendy and very wearable. She has some particularly lovely handbags by Ayayo (around 1,000kr) and leather outfits by K Bayashi. For those who are keen to stay looking young and hip, there are designs by Maria Sjödin, Ask Daddy, Jag and Branting.

❽ Judits Second Hand★★

Hornsgatan, 75
☎ 08 84 45 10
Open Mon.-Fri. 11am-7pm, Sat. 11am-4pm.

This large warehouse is full of second-hand designer clothes, mostly for women. If you want to have a good look round, you'll need to allow plenty of time for a really good rummage, and to try on some of the clothes. All the items are clean, in good condition and stylish, but you can't haggle on prices, so if you find some real gems, you'll have to be prepared to pay out.

❾ Wollmar Antik & Kuriosa★★

Wollmar Yxkullsgatan, 9
☎ 08 38 82 83
Open Mon.-Fri. noon-6pm, Sat. noon-4pm.

This place looks a bit like a garage, which is rather appropriate, since Peter Bäckström specialises in second-hand biker clothes and accessories, ranging from the 1930s to the present day. You'll find leather jackets and coats at attractive prices, alongside furniture, lamps and other items from the 1930s to the 1970s. And if you're looking for second-hand designer leather luggage, then Peter's your man.

❿ Teater Lasse I Parken★★★

Högalidsgatan, 56
☎ 08 669 04 20
Café & Restaurant: open every day 11am-8pm (Apr.-Oct.), weekends only during rest of year. Performances: 7.30pm (depending on weather, Apr.-Oct. only).

Mickael Reuterberg is a member of the Swedish National Theatre during most

of the year, but during the summer months the actor/director can be found at this open-air theatre. He has spent the warmer months in this lovely spot on Söder since 1986, during which time he has taken over the nearby restaurant, housed in a former tobacco hut, where he offers inclusive theatre and supper tickets. If you're expecting a traditional interpretation then be warned, works by playwrights such as Molière and Alan

⑪ CONTEMPORARY SILVERWARE★★★

There are two lovely shops and a studio selling delightful contemporary silverware (including jewellery and decorative items), perched neatly on Hornsgatan's 'hump'. Prices are relatively high, but the designs are stunning.

Metallum
Hornsgatan, 30
☎ 08 640 13 23
Open Tue. 11am-7pm, Wed.-Fri. 11am-6pm, Sat. 11am-4pm, Sun. noon-4pm

Efva Attling
Hornsgatan, 42
Open Mon.-Fri. 10am-6pm, Sat. 11am-3pm; July: Mon.-Fri. 10am-5.30pm.

Smide och Form
Hornsgatan, 38
Open Mon.-Thurs. 9am-5pm, Fri. 9am-3pm.

Ayckbourn are staged with a distinctly rock 'n' roll flavour that will outrage some and entertain others. You'll need to book in advance as the theatre only holds 150 spectators in the tent.

⑫ Carlshälls Gård★★
Långholmen
☎ 08 668 07 10
Open Mon.-Fri. 11.30am-2pm, 5-10pm (May-Sept.); closed July.

At the far end of Långholmen, you'll find this lovely house, built in 1838 for the director of the prison located on the island and later purchased by a large vodka manufacturer. Today, it's a lovely country restaurant with a pretty view over Lake Mälaren and the Smedsuddsbadet beach on the edge of Kungsholmen. At the weekends it plays host to chic weddings and smart private dinners.

⑬ Bysis★
Hornsgatan, 82b
☎ 08 84 59 10
Open Mon., Tue. & Thurs. 11am-11pm, Wed., Fri. & Sat. 11am-1am.

⑭ HORNSGATAN'S 'HUMP'

Despite work done in the 1950s to widen the street, Hornsgatan still retains an undeniable charm, largely due to its unusual 'hump' – a stretch that is still intact, complete with its ramp, which climbs up and then down again towards the street. The traffic is very heavy, but at times there's an eerie silence, which has made it a popular home for a number of artists' studios and galleries.

This building, dating from the late 18th century, was originally constructed as a workshop and home for a furrier. It later became a prison, before being turned into a psychiatric hospital. Today it has been converted into a charming restaurant, with a warm, country atmosphere and a lovely, welcoming fireplace, serving traditional Swedish and international cuisine. In the evenings, it turns into a friendly pub, and in the summer months, the courtyard is filled with rustic wooden benches and tables.

Östermalm and the History Museum

The eastern part of this district, once very poor, was rebuilt in the 19th century modelled along the lines of Paris. Today, it's a very smart area, with wide, tree-lined avenues bordered by embassy buildings and the homes of the wealthy. Thought by some to be part of the suburbs, the area is becoming increasingly lively as more and more trendy restaurants open their doors.

Kommendörsgatan
Grev Turegatan
Nybrogatan
Sibyllegatan
Jungfrugatan
Linnégatan
Grevgatan

❼ Östermalms Saluhall
Birger Jarlsgatan
Riddargatan
Artillerigatan
Storgatan
Historiska Museet ❶
Narvavägen
Linnégatan

❹ Kungl Dramatiska Teatern
Skeppargatan
Grevgatan
Styrmansgatan
Grev Magnig.
Storgatan
Strandvägen
Riddargatan
❺ ❷ ❻
Museispårvägen
Strandvägen
❸

❶ Historiska Museet ★★
Narvavägen, 13-17
☎ 08 519 556 00
Open every day 11am-5pm (15 May-14 Sept.), Tue.-Sun. 11am-5pm (15 Sept.-14 May); late night opening Thurs. to 8pm.
Entrance charge.

The Museum of National Antiquities covers 12,000 years of history. The ground floor houses early finds including Viking weapons, coins and boats. On the first floor are the Medieval Rooms, with sculpted wooden altarpieces, reconstructed sections of stave churches and examples of religious art. The basement is home to an underground vault, the Gold Room, with stunning 5th-century gold collars and fine pieces of jewellery and coins. If you're feeling peckish, you can have lunch in the café or the garden for 50kr. (See also p. 126.)

❷ Svenskt Tenn ★★★
Strandvägen, 5
☎ 08 670 16 00
Open Mon.-Fri. 10am-6pm, Sat. 10am-4pm.

'Swedish Pewter' was established in 1924 and is now internationally famous. Founded by Estrid Ericson and the Austrian architect and designer Josef Frank, Svenskt Tenn produces magnificent pieces of pewter and a whole host of functional and decorative items inspired by Josef Frank's designs. There are wonderful fabrics printed with colourful designs inspired by nature, and furniture and lamps that were synonymous with the Swedish Modern Style, so successful at the Universal Exhibition in Paris in 1937. This is a compulsory stop, offering no end of possible gifts to take home.

❸ STRANDVÄGEN★

At the start of the 20th century, Stockholm's ten wealthiest families moved into the sumptuous Art Nouveau buildings that line the city's most beautiful avenue. Strandvägen runs alongside Nybroviken pier, and from here you can cross a small bridge and arrive at the northern entrance to Djurgården.

❹ Kungl Dramatiska Teatern★★
Nybrogatan, 6
☎ 08 696 06 08
Guided visits Mon.-Fri. 3pm (Sept.-May), Sat. 3pm (rest of year); closed July.

This is Stockholm's showpiece theatre, located at the start of Strandvägen. It has a white marble façade and is a wonderful example of Art Nouveau architecture. Statues by Carl Milles stand either side of the steps and it has a marble foyer and an auditorium designed according to 17th-century tenets. While you're here you can visit the Pauli restaurant for a spot of refreshment (☎ 08 665 61 43, open Mon.-Fri. 11.30am-9pm, Sat.-Sun. 1-9pm) and sit on the terrace balcony overlooking the Nybroplan marina.

❺ Carl Malmsten★★
Strandvägen, 5b
Metro Kungsträdgården
☎ 08 23 33 80
Open Mon.-Fri. 10am-6pm, Sat. 10am-4pm.

Carl Malmsten is famous for his pale wood and painted wooden furniture, inspired by the rustic Swedish style, as well as for the furniture he designed for the town hall. Rugs by Märta Måås-Fjetterström are also on display here. These are quite remarkable works of art and further examples can be seen in the Stadshuset and at Arlanda airport. Prices, however, are exorbitant, probably since only 30 pieces are made per year.

❻ T-Bar★★
Hotell Diplomat
Strandvägen, 7c
☎ 08 459 68 00
Open every day 6.30am-midnight.

The T-Bar is a very chic spot to meet for a light lunch or at teatime. Renovated in 2000 by the architect G Palmstierna, it's popular with the trendy youth of Stockholm, who meet up to enjoy an aperitif in the atmospheric music lounge. If you find a window table, you can enjoy a view of the water at the same time.

❼ Östermalms Saluhall★★★
Östermalmstorg (on the corner of Humlegårdsgatan and Nybrogatan)
Open Mon.-Thurs. 9.30am-6pm, Fri. 9.30am-6.30pm, Sat. 9.30am-2pm.

Östermalmstorg, the square to the west of the theatre, is the site of the rather ritzy Östermalms Saluhall, a covered market hall housed in a rust-coloured brick building with a slate steeple. The interior is late 19th-century in style and is like a huge delicatessen, with each stall selling fresh produce and food, served either at the counter or at the small tables dotted around. It's a great place for Saturday lunch, but keep an eye on the prices, as it's quite expensive.

Around Stureplan

Stureplan stands at the heart of the city, at the intersection of the large, smart, avenues like Birger Jarlsgatan and the less exclusive streets such as Kungsgatan. It's busy and lively both day and night, and makes a perfect departure point for shopping expeditions in the surrounding streets, as well as wild evenings out in the local bars and clubs which are always buzzing.

RUNEBERGSPLAN
Karlavägen
Engelbrektsgatan
Kungliga Humlegården
Kungliga Biblioteket **2**
Birger Jarlsgatan
Sturegatan
Brahegatan
Humlegårdsgatan **3**
Kungsg. STUREPLAN **1**
Norrlandsgatan
Grev Turegatan
4 Sturebadet **6**
Biblioteksgatan
Smålandsgatan
Riddargatan
Birger Jarlsgatan
Hamng. **Hallwylska Museet** **5**
Nybrog.
Sibylleg.
Museispårvägen
Kungsträdgårds.

❶ Stureplan

Despite being rather unattractive, the popular *Svampen* ('mushroom') building, erected in 1937 by Holger Blom and restored around ten years ago, is still where night owls like to meet up. Just opposite on the square, at no. 10, you can see the wonderful Danelisuka Huset, built in 1900 by Erik Josephson in flamboyant neo-Gothic style, as a reaction against the Art Nouveau style prevalent at the time.

❷ Kungliga Biblioteket★★

Library open Mon.-Thurs. 9am-8pm, café open Mon.- Fri. 9am-4pm (1 Jan.-mid June, 13 Aug.-31 Dec.); library open Mon.-Thurs. 9am-6pm, café open Mon.-Fri. 9am-4pm (mid June-mid Aug.). Free entrance.

At the centre of the lovely Humlegården with its 100-year old trees, stands the Royal Library, built between the end of the 19th century and 1997. Behind its façade is the marble hall and the reading room that dates from

the 19th century, which has been preserved intact, complete with metal pillars decorated with *trompe l'oeil* images from Ancient Greece. At the back is a rather

stunning glass stairwell, a recent addition, which leads down to an underground auditorium.

❸ Wok Away★★

Kunglika Humlegården Open every day for lunch, 11.30am-4pm, and for dinner and bar, 4pm-1am.

Edward Lundberg, the owner of Wok Away, had a very precise concept in mind when he opened this

lovely open-air restaurant at the edge of the Humlegården garden. All the food is stir-fried (in a wok – no surprises there), in a wooden hut, from where you can buy your takeaway lunch or dinner (set meals cost 60kr and 90kr). During the summer months a large terrace is set up outside, and in the evening it becomes a very pleasant club playing jazz music.

THE KINGDOM OF SHOPPING★★

All the luxury shops and trendy Swedish designer boutiques are concentrated in just a few streets – Birger Jarlsgatan, Grev Turegatan, Nybrogatan, Biblioteksgatan, Mäster Samuelsgatan and Jakobsbergsgatan. Once you've visited the Sturegallerian shopping mall on Grev Turegatan, often frequented by the Swedish royal family, check out the less exclusive, more popular shopping street of Kungsgatan.

❹ Sturebadet★★★

Sturegallerian, 36
☎ **08 545 015 00**
Open Mon.-Fri. 6.30am-10pm, Sat.-Sun. 9am-7pm (25 June-19 Aug. open Mon.-Fri. 6.30am-9pm, Sat.-Sun. 9am-6pm), closed one week in July.

This swimming pool, built in the late 19th century in the Sturegallerian, serves as a very smart beauty spa. In fact, it's Stockholm's most chic venue for beauty treatments, facials, massages etc. If you're not in the mood to be pampered, however, you can always ask politely at reception for a quick guided tour. With a bit of luck, you may get to see the turquoise mosaic pool located in the lovely curved wooden gallery, which also houses the treatment rooms. There's a distinct oriental feel to the place.

❺ Hallwylska Museet★★

Hamngatan, 4
☎ **08 519 555 90**
Guided tours only, Tue.-Sun. 1pm (in English).

Countess Wilhelmina von Hallwyl, a wealthy patron of the arts, collected some wonderful paintings, sculpture, silverware and ceramics, which are displayed here. The house was built in the late 19th century and has been preserved intact.

Today, the Baroque sitting room houses various treasures including a Steinway piano. In the summer, the Renaissance-style inner courtyard hosts classical music concerts, while in the cooler winter months, performances of Strindberg's *Fröken Julie* (Miss Julie) are occasionally held in the kitchen.

❻ Svenkst Paper★

Birger Jarlsgatan, 23
☎ **08 772 32 75**
Open Mon.-Fri. 10am-5.30pm.

This professional showroom is simply filled with different types of paper. Open to the public, it has a huge range of wonderful Swedish paper in a medley of colours, as well as a selection of rare paper from Asia and in particular, Tibet.

From Kungsträdgården to Hötorget

Konserthuset

Olof Palmes gatan
Apelbergsgatan
Kungsgatan
Drottninggatan
Malmskillnadsgatan
Sveavägen
Mäster Samuelsgatan
Regeringsgatan
Hamngatan
Västra Trädgårdsg.
Kungsträdgårdsg.

Kulturhuset

Malmtorgsg.
Drottninggatan
Regeringsgatan
Jakobsgatan
Fredsgatan
Strömgatan
Norrbro
Riksg.

Kungsträdgården
Operan

This area offers a fascinating view of Stockholm in its various stages of development, from the 17th century right up to the 21st century. There are many interesting places to explore between the Old Town and the City, from the small Kungsträdgården park to the impressive Hötorget Square, as well as Sergels Torg, a lasting symbol of the dramatic changes that took place in Sweden during the 1970s.

❶ Kungsträdgården★

Under the watchful eyes of Carl XII and Carl XIII, whose statues stand on either side of the Molin fountain, Stockholm's oldest garden provides a popular meeting place for families. In the summer months, an outdoor stage is erected for jazz concerts, live theatre and other performances. In winter, the central pond becomes an ice-skating rink, whilst street entertainment takes place all year round. There's always something going on here.

❷ Operan (Opera House)★★
Karl XII Torget
☎ **08 791 43 00.**

This impressive 19th-century building is an institution in Stockholm and a perfect

example of the academic style that prevailed at the time. Axel Anderberg was commissioned to design it as a replacement for the former Baroque opera house, built in the previous century. The extension to the opera house, completed in the 1950s on the Kungsträdgården side, houses four restaurants, including the wonderful but very expensive Operakällaren and the celebrated Café Opera.

❸ Kulturhuset★★★
Sergels Torg
☎ **08 508 315 08**
Guided tours Wed. 11.30am and Sun. 3pm.
Free entrance.

Built by Peter Celsing between 1968 and 1973, this vast five-storey cultural centre stands as a stark contrast to the nearby

temples of shopping. Behind its glass façade are three galleries that hold exhibitions of photography, the plastic arts, multimedia, fashion and design. The Hörsalen auditorium offers a varied programme in contemporary dance and theatre, as well as providing activities for children, an interactive play and education area, café and cybercafé.

Sveavägen there are five new buildings designed in the same style. They proved to be highly controversial among the defenders of traditional architectural styles.

❺ Soup
Sveavägen, 30
☎ 08 458 002 58.

Kia Andersson has come up with an idea that she's planning to develop in other European countries – a soup bar where you choose your own ingredients. Whether you pick New Dehli, Tokyo, San Francisco, Bangkok or Cairo, you won't pay more than around 50kr.

❻ Zenit★
Sveavägen, 20
☎ 08 698 57 40
Open Mon.-Fri. 8am-8pm, Sat. 11am-6pm, Sun. noon-6pm.

This internet café is home to a small multicultural, multi-ethnic centre, supported by the Swedish government and run by a group of young

❹ Sergelstorg and Sveavägen★
On Stockholm's busiest square, opposite Sveavägen, stands a tall, glass obelisk designed by Edvin Öhrström, which is particularly impressive at night when lit up against the dark sky. The area around Klarabergsgatan and Hamngatan is known locally as 'the City' and is the newest district in the Swedish capital. It's home to the huge NK and Åhléns stores, and on

❽ BOUTIQUE SPORTIF★
Oxtorgsgatan, 6
☎ 08 411 12 13
Open Mon.-Fri. noon-7pm, Sat. noon-5pm.

If you want to replenish your stocks of US streetwear whilst you're in town, this is the place to come. Stussy International, T5S, Duffer – all the great labels are here, in an atmosphere that's definitely 'urban jungle'. The walls are covered in interesting, if unintelligible, Swedish graffiti, and you can listen to the rhythms of Bob Marley as you try on your potential purchases. It's quite a place.

performers. A forum for discussion and exchange, it's also a venue for world music concerts, theatrical events and interactive or thematic exhibitions. Young people like to drop in here for a drink or snack in the friendly, relaxed atmosphere.

❼ Konserthuset★★
Hötorget
☎ 08 786 02 00.

This blue neo-Classical building, the work of Ivar Tengbom, hosts the annual Nobel Prize ceremony, which is followed by a gala dinner held in the town hall. Outside, you'll find the impressive bronze *Orpheus* sculptures by Carl Milles, the originals of which are in Millesgården to the northeast of the city.

Around the Strindberg Museum

Just a few minutes' walk from the centre, the top end of Norrmalm splits into two – the residential and the commercial districts. After a compulsory visit to the Strindberg museum, a cult figure in Sweden, carry on along Drottninggatan for a spot of shopping, to visit a café, or even to go for a swim at the Centralbadet.

❶ Strindbergs-museet★★

Drottninggatan, 85 (4th flr)
☎ **08 411 53 54**
Open Tue. noon-7pm (June-Aug. noon-4pm), Wed.-Sun. noon-4pm.
Entrance charge.

This Art Nouveau building, named the 'Blue Tower' by Strindberg himself because of its azure stairwell, was his last home in Stockholm. Take the beautiful lift up and the stairs down, to avoid missing the lovely motifs on the windows. The museum houses a reconstruction of the apartment where Strindberg lived from 1908 to 1912, including his study, with the venetian blinds and heavy curtains still closed against the sunlight, and a library where his books and correspondence are displayed. You can also see paintings and photographs of actors who have played parts in his works. Concerts are sometimes held in the museum and are worth going to if you get the chance.

❷ Souk★

Drottninggatan, 104
☎ **08 411 89 11**
Open Tue.-Fri. 11am-6pm, Sat. 11am-4pm.

Take a well-deserved rest and pop into Souk for a refreshing cup of mint tea and a selection of tasty Eastern pastries, especially if you fancy a change from all the Swedish goodies on offer. It also sells a selection of attractive Moroccan decorative items such as mirrors, tiles, fabrics, mosaic tables and lanterns.

❸ Tegnérlunden★

This pretty garden, perched on the top of a hill is surrounded by 19th-century bourgeois apartments. It has a lovely view over Kungsholmen and is home to a magnificent statue of Strindberg by the sculptor Carl Eldh, depicting him as

Prometheus with his hands bound, which you may have already spotted from the 'Blue Tower'. It was erected in 1942 as a tribute to the political courage of the author.

AUGUST STRINDBERG

Strindberg was born in Stockholm in 1849 and died there in 1912. He spent many years of his life in France, and his plays are still enjoyed in many countries, in particular *Miss Julie*. He is Sweden's most provocative and influential playwright, and although he never received a Nobel prize because of his socialist political commitment, he was awarded the 'anti-Nobel prize' by workers and students in 1912. He was also a talented artist as witnessed in an exhibition dedicated to him in 2001.

❹ Centralbadet★★★
Drottninggatan, 88
☎ 08 545 213 00
Open Mon.-Fri. 6am-9pm (gym opens at 10am), Sat.-Sun. 8am-9pm (sauna and jacuzzi close at 9.30pm), last admission 8.30pm; closed Sun. in July and public hols.

This magnificent pool complex, built in 1904 in Art Nouveau style, has retained much of its original atmosphere and is a fabulous place to come for a swim. The whole place is dedicated to the art of wellbeing and relaxation, and you can easily spend an entire day here. There's a restaurant, pool bar and sun terrace where you can soak up some rays (summer only). You can swim, enjoy a range of body treatments or

join the locals in one of the three saunas or the jacuzzi – usually a family affair – but watch out for kiddies hour in the pool!

❺ Ordning & Reda★★
Drottninggatan, 82
☎ 08 10 84 96
Open Mon.-Fri. 10am-6pm, Sat. 10am-4pm, Sun. noon-3pm.

This shop is a haven for stationery lovers, boasting a fabulous collection of writing paper, envelopes, pens, crayons and ballpoints available in a rainbow of colours. The attractive range of paper is manufactured in Sweden, although there are outlets outside the country. There are some lovely hand-bound photo albums and plastic-covered notebooks decorated with pretty motifs.

❻ STHLM: Kaffé med Mjolk
Drottninggatan, 73c
☎ 08 22 56 66
Open Mon.-Fri. 8am-8pm, Sat.-Sun. 10am-6pm.

This friendly, atmospheric café is good place to come for a drink or a spot of lunch in between shopping expeditions along Drottninggatan, one of Stockholm's busiest streets. The walls are decorated with the work of young Swedish artists and the youthful owner, Elias, is very welcoming.

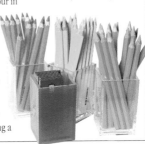

Skeppsholmen, the island of museums

The island of Skeppsholmen, the 18th-century royal naval base, is home to several of Stockholm's largest museums. Away from the bustle of city life, it can be reached via the Skeppsholmsbron metal bridge that links it to the island of Blasieholmen. Facing the Royal Palace you can see the National Museum and the Grand Hotel, where winners of the Nobel Prize and their families traditionally stay.

Hovslagarg.

National Art Museum
6

Skeppsholmsbron

Östasiatiska Museet
1

2 **Moderna Museet**
4

5 3

Arkitekturmuseet

Svensksundsv.

7

Långa Raden

Södra Brobanken

Ostra Kastelholmskajen

Open Tue.-Thurs. 11am-8pm, Fri.-Sun. 11am-6pm. Entrance charge.

Opened in 1998, this wonderful if controversial building was designed by Spanish architect Rafael Moneo and houses both the Museum of Modern Art and the Museum of Architecture.

❶ Östasiatiska Museet (Museum of Far Eastern Antiquities)★

Skeppsholmen*
☎ 08 519 557 50
www.mfea.se
Open Tue. noon-8pm, Wed.-Sun. noon-5pm. Entrance charge.

Housed in a former military building, constructed in the 13th century by Tessin the Younger for the royal guard of Carl XII, this museum contains archaeological finds from all over Asia dating back as far as the Stone Age. The Chinese ceramics (from 7th century onwards) and the 6th-century wooden statues of Buddha and Shiva are quite fascinating.
*Closed for renovation until summer 2003.

❷ Moderna Museet (Museum of Modern Art)★★★

Skeppsholmen*
☎ 08 51 95 52 00
www.modernamuseet.se

The Moderna Museet has an impressive collection of art by 20th-century masters, such as Picasso, Matisse, Penn, Warhol and Pollock, together with the work of contemporary

❼ Svensk Form, the Future of Design★★★

Holmamiralens Väg, 2
☎ **08 463 31 30**
www.svenskform.se
Open Tue.-Thurs. noon-7pm, Fri.-Sun. noon-5pm.
Entrance charge.

Founded in 1845, Svensk Form is the descendant of the Svenska Slöjdföreningen (The Society of Crafts and Industrial Design), which organised Stockholm's Great Exhibition of 1930, which heralded the birth of Swedish industrial design. It has its own gallery on the island of Skeppsholmen and publishes a design magazine as well as a guide to design addresses in Stockholm. Run by the state, it also awards an annual prize for excellence in Swedish design.

artists. It boasts the world's best collection of Swedish art, with collections changing each year. There's also a financial programme to support today's talented artists. *Until autumn 2003 the museum will be located at Klarabergsviadukten, 61 (near the Central Station). Entrance is free while renovations are in progress.

❸ Arkitekturmuseet (Museum of Architecture)★

Skeppsholmen*
☎ **08 858 72 70 00**
www.arkitekturmuseet.se
Open Tue.-Thurs. 11am-8pm, Fri.-Sun. 11am-6pm.
Entrance charge.

The Museum of Architecture is housed in a fabulous building with its permanent exhibition giving you an excellent idea of Swedish architectural design from its early beginnings to the present day. There are also temporary exhibitions on architecture, photography, design and urban art.
*Until autumn 2003 exhibitions will be held at Fredsgatan, 12 (opening times as above) and Skeppsholm church (open Tues.-Sun. 1-5pm). Entrance is free while renovations are in progress.

❹ Kantin Moneo★★
Opening times as museum.

The museum café, designed by the celebrated Swede Thomas Sandell, is stunningly decorated in red and white. For a fabulous view over Djurgården and the Vasa museum, head for the terrace.

❺ Museum bookshop★★
Opening times as museum

Before you leave the museum, visit the wonderful bookshop which boasts a multilingual collection of books on architecture, photography and

design, as well as a great collection of posters and postcards and a children's section with books and toys.

❻ National Art Museum★★★

Blasieholmshamnen (just before Skeppsholmsbron)
☎ **08 519 543 00**
Open Tue.-Thurs. 10am-9pm, Wed., Fri.-Sun. 10am-5pm.
Entrance charge.

This amazing museum, built in the 19th century, faces the Royal Palace and is the largest in Sweden. It houses an impressive collection of European fine and applied arts from the late middle ages to the 19th century, with a fascinating exhibition covering a hundred years of Swedish design (1900-2000). There are also paintings and sculptures, with some stunning pieces by Swedish artists from the 18th and 19th centuries. (See also p. 127.)

Kungsholmen, home to the Stadshuset

The island of Kungsholmen is dominated by the City Hall and marks the starting point of Lake Mälaren. It is divided into two parts: a chic, but relatively quiet residential area (although it does have a few nice surprises), and the popular Rålambshov park that leads to Smedsuddsbadet, where you can take a swim in the lake and enjoy the wonderful views.

❶ Stadshuset (City Hall)★★★

Hantverkargatan, 1
☎ 08 508 290 58
Open every day (except Christmas Eve, Christmas Day and New Year's Day)
Guided tours only, 10am and noon (plus 11am and 2pm, 1 June-31 Aug.).
Entrance charge.

Built between 1911 and 1923 by architect Ragnar Östberg, the City Hall is a fine example of the 'National Romantic' style and one of Stockholm's modern landmarks, showcasing the considerable skill of Sweden's artisans. You're likely to be joined by a couple of coach loads of tourists but be patient – like you, they are here to admire the strangely

named 'Blue Hall' (blue in name only), in which the Nobel Prize banquet is held and the equally stunning Golden Hall. (See also p. 133.)

❷ The Stadshuset Tower★★★

Open every day 10am-4.30pm (May-Sept.),
Sat.-Sun. 10am-4pm (Apr.).

Make sure you wear comfortable shoes – the lift only takes you half way up this 106-metre (348-foot) square tower, built entirely in red brick. To reach the top, where the steeple sports the Swedish royal emblem of three crowns, you need to climb a seemingly endless staircase. The view from the top is awesome and at noon you can hear the bells chime.

❸ Papphanssons soppor★

Wargentinsgatan, 3
☎ 08 654 56 10
Open Mon.- Thurs. 11am-8pm, Fri. 11am-6pm.

Catrin and Julia will give you a warm welcome in their small but friendly café, where only one dish appears on the menu – soup. Each day they

make seven different types plus a goulash, and the menu changes weekly. It's a great spot to enjoy an inexpensive lunch (around 55kr) and it's usually full of locals.

❹ R.O.O.M★★
Alströmergatan, 20
☎ **08 692 50 00**
Open Mon.-Fri. 10am-7pm, Sat. 10am-5pm, Sun. noon-4pm; in summer (June to mid-Aug.) Mon.-Fri. 10am-6pm, Sat. 10am-3pm.

Fans of the Conran Shop and Habitat will love this place. It's a huge glass-roofed warehouse selling everything you could possibly want (if not necessarily need) for the home, from simple and reasonably-priced cutlery, to colourful crockery and luxury sofas. Not all the products are made in Sweden, but they are generally attractive designer items. After carrying out a thorough inspection of their entire stock, you can sit down and enjoy a glass of fresh fruit juice on the pretty terrace.

❺ Syskonen Linnmans, Salt & Sött★★
Pipersgatan, 14
☎ **08 650 58 04**
Open Mon.-Fri. 11am-6pm, Sat. noon-4pm.

If you're feeling a bit peckish, pop into this Italian ice-cream parlour, run by brother and sister duo Anders and Asså, who took over the shop, first established way back in 1920, just six years ago. It now serves a wonderful range

of ice-creams and sorbets, with a hundred-or-so flavours to choose from, such as saffron and cardamom, raspberry sorbet, and for the more adventurous, fläderblom-saft, made from a flower that grows only in Scandinavia.

❻ Schalin★
Bergsgatan, 9
☎ **08 653 16 25**
Open Mon.-Fri. noon-6pm, Sat. noon-4pm.

In his boutique-studio, stylist Johan Schalin makes super trendy clothes for men and women who want to stand out

from the crowd. His sweatshirts with extra-long sleeves are a bargain at just 395kr, and look out for his shimmery nylon blazers, denim skirts with pink zips and his

black vinyl belts. He also sells rather lovely boots with very pointy toes.

❼ RÅLAMBSHOV-PARKEN

Created in 1935, this park stretches from the Tranebergsbron bridge in the west, which leads to Drottningholm, to the Smedsuddsvägen coastal road to the east, and is bordered by a pretty marina. As soon as the first rays of sun appear, the locals head here to bronze their bodies or venture bravely into the waters of Lake Mälaren for a swim. To the south of the island, Mariebergsparken and Smedsuddsbadet beach are even more popular. The view of Långholmen is also quite spectacular from here.

Djurgården, the pleasure island

Stockholmers are proud of their urban parkland, Ekoparken, the first European national park to be located in the heart of a city. The island of Djurgården, which forms part of the park, was once home to the royal hunting grounds. Today, families flock here at weekends, entering through the elegant and decorative wrought-iron 'Blue Gate', to enjoy cultural events and other forms of entertainment. It goes to show that you don't need to leave the city to enjoy the sea and the countryside.

Strandvägen
Nordiska Museet
Junibacken ⑨ ⑤
Vasamuseet ⑧
Liljevalchs Konsthall
⑩
Gröna Lund
⑫
Tramway 7
Rosendalsvägen
⑪
Skansen ①
Sirishovsv
Djurgårdsslätten
⑫
De Besches Väg
③ ②
Rosendals Trädgard
Manillavägen
Prins Eugens Waldemarsudde
⑥

❶ Skansen★★

Main entrance on Djurgårdsslätten
☎ 08 442 80 00
Park: open every day (exc. 24 Dec.) 10am-8pm; June-Aug. 10am-10pm; Sept. 10am-5pm; Historic houses: open May-Sept. 11am-5pm; Oct.-Apr. 11am-3pm; Shop: open every day 11am-5pm; Jan-Feb. 11am-4pm, June-Aug. 11am-7pm. Entrance charge.

Skansen, built in 1891, was the first ever open-air museum, and today comprises 150 reconstructed buildings documenting some 500 years of Swedish history. Founded by Artur Hazelius, it shows how people used to live, with its own town, windmills, farms and craftsmen's workshops, laid out region-by-region, complete with animals and people dressed in period costume. Great attention is paid to detail and it makes an enjoyable outing, particularly if you have young children. (See also p. 128.)

❷ Rosendals Trädgård★★★

Rosendalsterrassen, 12
☎ 08 545 812 70
Greenhouses & shop: open all year Tue.-Sun. 10am-4pm, 1 May-30 Sept. every day 10am-6pm; Café: open all year Tue.-Sun. 11am-4pm, 1 May-30 Sept. every day 11am-5pm.

At the heart of the park, near the small Rosendals royal

pavilion, you'll come across a wonderful kitchen garden and orchard, where everything is grown organically. There's a lovely café serving 100% organic food as well as a shop where you can buy all your organic produce on the spot. A range of plants, ceramic and terracotta pots and gardening tools are also for sale in the neighbouring greenhouses.

you can sit on the terrace, listen to the birdsong and choose something tasty from the unpretentious and delicious, traditional Swedish menu.

❹ Liljevalchs Konsthall★★★
Djurgårdsvägen, 60
☎ 08 508 313 30
Open Tue.-Sun. 11am-5pm; late night opening Sept.-May, Tue. & Thurs. to 8pm.
Entrance charge.

Constructed between 1913 and 1916 by Carl Bergsten, thanks to a donation by industrialist Carl Fredrich Liljevalchs, the quality of the exhibits and the beautiful architecture of this museum make it well worth a visit. It illustrates art during the transition between the 'National Romantic' style at the beginning of the 20th century and the more classical traditions of the 1920s. Its huge rooms, bathed in natural light, are home to some excellent examples of 20th-century paintings, sculpture and photography. There's a good restaurant in the garden.

GARDEN DELIGHT

In the 18th century it was fashionable in high society to enjoy events in the Rosendals gardens. Today you can do the same during spring and summer, when gardening courses, concerts, literary evenings and exhibitions are held in the royal pavilion. In autumn you can come and pick the flowers and make up your own bouquet, priced by weight.

❸ Rosendals Wärdshus★★
Rosendalsterrassen, 3
☎ 08 661 39 70
Open every day 11am-10pm.

This is the place to come for Sunday brunch. It's a lovely restaurant, housed in a greenhouse on the top of Rosendals, with a great view over the gardens. In summer,

❺ Nordiska Museet★
Djurgårdsvägen, 6
☎ 08 519 560 00
Open Tue.-Sun. 10am-5pm (Wed. to 8pm), closed Mon.
Entrance charge.

The impressive Nordic museum, constructed at the beginning of the 20th century in the Swedish Renaissance style, was originally meant to be even larger than the grand edifice you see today. Like the Skansen museum, it was the inspiration of Artur Hazelius, whose mission was to bring together images of Swedish life from different periods of history. There are interesting collections of furniture, costume and tableware, whilst the third floor of the museum

...is dedicated to Strindberg and houses temporary exhibitions on popular contemporary Swedish culture. Carl Milles' phenomenal statue of Gustav Vasa, the 16th-century king who drove out the Danes, graces the main hall. (See also p. 129.)

⑥ Prins Eugens Waldemarsudde★★

Prins Eugens Väg, 6
☎ 08 545 837 00
Open Tue.-Sun. 11am-5pm (Thurs. to 8pm); Park open daily, all year round. Guided tour in English: Tues.-Fri. 3pm (June-Aug.). Entrance charge.

Nestled in a bay lies the retreat that once belonged to Prince Eugen (1864-1947), younger brother of King Gustav. A haven of peace and culture,

the house of this lover of art, botany and music, has recently been renovated and now displays his collection of 19th-century paintings and sculptures. You can also explore the wonderful terraced gardens that lead down to the sea, dominated by a linseed oil mill, a landmark for boats on their way to the archipelago. (See also p. 136.)

⑦ Thielska Galleriet★★

Blockhusudden
☎ 08 662 58 84
Open Mon.-Sat. noon-4pm, Sun. 1-4pm. Entrance charge.

This house, built at the start of the 20th century by Ferdinand Boberg for the banker Ernest Thiel, stands at the far eastern end of Djurgården and houses Thiel's impressive art collection. There are many

⑪ OUTSIDE IN DJURGÅRDS-BRUNNSVIKEN
☎ 08 660 57 57
Open end Apr.-end Sept. every day 9am-9pm.

Anyone can enjoy a romantic walk along Rosendalsvägen, but if you're feeling energetic, you can cycle, go on rollerblades or even take a pedalo. The narrow channel between Djurgården and Ladugårdsgärdet is known as Djurgårdsbrunnsviken and is a popular area for swimming in summer and skating in winter, when it freezes over. It leads to the sea and the start of the archipelago. Equipment can be hired by the hour, half day or whole day, from the Djurgårdsbrons Sjöcafé at the entrance to the park (on left past bridge). Bikes cost 250kr, rollerblades 200kr, canoes 300kr, rowing boats 400kr, pedalos 400kr and kayaks 500kr (prices based on a whole day's hire).

Swedish works commissioned by the patron himself, such as domestic interiors by Carl Larsson, landscapes by Bruno Liljefors and melancholic canvasses by Eugene Jansson.

❽ Vasamuseet★★★
Galärvarnet
☎ 08 519 548 00
Open every day mid-June to mid-Aug. 9.30am-7pm, mid-Aug. to mid-June 10am-5pm, (Wed. to 8pm). Entrance charge.

One of Stockholm's real treasures and an absolute must, this museum houses the magnificent Vasa warship, built on the orders of King Gustav II Adolf, and raised along with 12,000 objects from Stockholm's harbour in 1961.

Långstrump), the endearing character created by Sweden's popular children's author, Astrid Lindgren. Pippi, with her red hair and long thin legs, always wore stockings that didn't match. It's a great place for children as well as

adults and children alike. It can be reached by road or via the red and yellow ferry from Skeppsbrokajen. The most hair-raising ride is the *Fritt Fall*, the Free Fall Power Tower, which treats you to an 80-metre (262-foot) vertical drop in just over six seconds.

You might want to give it a miss if you are feeling fragile or have just had lunch!

❿ Take the tram
Take tram no. 7 from the town centre to Djurgården, the only one still in use with its unique slate blue carriage. It leaves every 12 minutes and connects Norrmalmstorg square, near the Nybroviken quay, with Oakhill, close to Prince Eugen's house. The Rullande Café, a more touristy option, follows the same route, but only runs at weekends. Recognisable by its distinctive purple and yellow carriages, it leaves every 35 minutes and costs 45kr, coffee and cake included.

It sank on its maiden voyage in 1628 and spent over 300 years in the silt of the sea bed. Dramatically displayed in half-light to prevent further deterioration, the sheer size of the ship and the beauty of its carvings are quite breathtaking. (See also p. 130.)

❾ Junibacken★★
Djurgården, next to the Vasamuseet
☎ 08 587 230 00
Open July every day 10am-8pm, Aug. 10am-5pm.

This museum is dedicated to Pippi Longstocking (*Pippi*

nostalgic parents, who can relive her adventures by boarding the mini train that takes you to Pippi's home and allows you to meet some of the author's other characters.

❿ Gröna Lund★
Djurgårdsfärjan
☎ 08 587 501 00
Website: www.tivoli.se
Open 1 May to mid-Sept., opening times vary. Entrance charge.

Gröna Lund is Stockholm's Tivoli Gardens and is the place to come in search of a thrill or two – suitable for

A tour of the archipelago

With 24,000 islands, some little more than uninhabitable rocks, the archipelago offers all the delights of outdoor living, just moments from the city gates. Whilst chic Swedes enjoy the marina and regattas of Sandhamn, others prefer the historical town of Vaxholm with its 17th-century fort, and nature lovers, of course, are in paradise just about anywhere. In summer, boats ensure daily communication between the city centre and the islands.

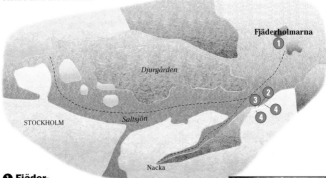

❶ Fjäder-holmarna★★★

Ferry leaves every 60 mins. 10am-8pm from Strandvägen (on the corner with Skeppargatan).

Fjäderholmarna – the Feather Islands – are the closest group of islands in the archipelago, lying just 25 minutes from the city centre. On the main island you can get a real idea of how Swedes spend their holidays. The grey rocks are covered in green vegetation and the area is dotted with red wooden houses with black, pointed roofs and pretty gardens. Here and there you'll see people enjoying a spot of fishing.

The workshops★★
Open every day 10.30am-5.15pm (end Apr.-mid Sept.).

During the summer months, artists and craftsmen (and women) share studio-boutiques on the southern coast of the island. Their work is generally stylish and contemporary, and the pieces make ideal, unusual gifts to take home. You'll find glassblowers, potters, weavers

nails. The collection ranges from a 1928 rowing boat, a popular model for travelling around the city, to the yachts of the 1950s and the first off-shore boats.

Fjäderholmarnas Krog och Magasin★★
Stora Fjäderholmen
☎ 08 718 33 55
Open every day noon-midnight.

This lovely restaurant is located in a huge wooden building on the eastern coast of the island. There's a choice of places to enjoy your meal – in the dining room, on the veranda, the terrace or the mezzanine. The decor is

simple and stylish, with grey-stained wooden walls, crisp linen tablecloths, comfortable cushion-covered sofas and sea-blue curtains. The food is principally fish-based and comprises traditional dishes from the archipelago.

❷ Nacka Strand
On your way to or from Fjäderholmarna, you may want to stop off at Nacka Strand – home to such major telecommunications companies as Ericsson or Telia (one of Sweden's largest

and fabric designers, and there's an art gallery and a forge to look round. There's plenty to keep you occupied.

Museiföreningen Sveriges Fritidsbåtar★
Open every day 10.30am-5.15pm.
Free entrance.

This small museum is definitely worth a visit if you're interested in the history of boat making or boat design. Housing a

handful of vessels made at the beginning of the 20th century, you can see some interesting examples of how boats used to be made from strips of wood held together with copper

❹ J★★
Augustendalvägen, 52
☎ 08 601 30 25
Open Mon.-Fri. 11.30am-midnight, Sat.-Sun. noon-midnight.

This quayside restaurant, popular with business-men during the week and wealthy Stockholmers at the weekends, has a blue and white interior and serves an international cuisine. If you want to keep costs down, just enjoy a glass of wine on the terrace (meals can be quite pricey). The J Hotel is a haven of tranquillity, with rooms overlooking pretty, green areas. The decor has a nautical theme and the atmosphere is friendly and welcoming. Rooms cost 1,595-3,395kr, with special deals available in summer.

operators) – and enjoy a walk along the jetty or among the trees. At lunchtime it's popular with yuppies and businessmen seeking a breath of fresh air.

❸ Gud på Himmelsbågen★★★

This magnificent sculpture, a claw-shaped vertical piece of steel topped with the figure of a boy, marks the entrance to the harbour. The original was designed by Carl Milles in 1946 to celebrate the formation of the United Nations and now stands in Millesgården. This, however, is a replica of the original and is the work of the American, Marshall M Fredericks, who helped the Swedish master sculptor for many years. It was unveiled in 1996.

Hagaparken, something for everyone

This magnificent park is located in the northern part of the city and is the perfect place to relax and have a picnic or go exploring. Highlights include the exotic botanical gardens, Gustav III's pavilion and the magnificent Roman war tents which are part of the Haga Parkmuseum. It takes just over 15 minutes to get to from the centre, on the no. 46 bus, or the no. 515 from Odenplan to Haga Södra or Haga Norra.

3 Fjärils Fågelhuset

2 Haga Parkmuseum

Slottsruinen

4

6 Ekotemplet

5 Gustav III's Paviljong

Brunnsviken

Hagaparken

1

7 Kinesika Pagoden

Haga Forum

8

9 Stallmästare-gården

❶ The park★★★

It was the erudite King Gustav III who commissioned the park in the 18th century, and it was his favourite architect, Fredrik Magnus Piper, who built the many pavilions. Unfortunately, the king never saw the work completed and after his assassination the project was halted. The remaining buildings still stand in this vast English-style park that now forms part of the Ekoparken. (See also p. 137.)

Swim, ski, sledge or skate★★★

This spot, to the west of the bay of Brunnsviken, is popular with Stockholmers all year round. In summer they swim in the sea, venture out in canoes or enjoy a jog or walk along the complete 10-km (6-mile) route. In winter, they don somewhat warmer attire and indulge in a spot of ice-skating, tobogganing or cross-country skiing.

❷ Haga Parkmuseum★★

☎ 08 402 61 30
Open 15 May-31 Aug.
Tue.-Sun. noon-4pm.
Free entrance.

Here you'll find replicas of Roman war tents, the Koppartälten, built in 1787 for the king's guards out of copper and decorated with blue and yellow trompe l'oeil images. To the left, the Haga Parkmuseum is home to a model of the completed royal castle. To the right, in the centre, is the Värdshuset Koppartälten café (☎ 08 27 70 02, open every day 11am-3pm) where you can buy a picnic basket.

9 STALLMÄSTARE-GÅRDEN
Norrtull
☎ 08 610 13 00.

Housed in Stockholm's oldest inn, built in the 17th century, is one of the city's finest restaurants. The building has retained much of its original charm, boasting a traditional, rustic interior. In 2000, a 49-room hotel opened under the same roof, its construction having been carefully monitored by locals concerned about its heritage. It offers a remarkable view over the lake and has a wonderful aromatic herb garden.

3 Fjärils and Fågelhuset★
☎ 08 730 39 81
Open Apr.-Sept. Tue.-Fri. 10am-4pm, Sat.-Sun. 11am-5.30pm; Oct.-Mar. Tue.-Fri. 10am-3pm, Sat.-Sun. 11am-4pm. Entrance charge.

This exotic attraction is great for families. A succession of glasshouses shelters a Japanese

garden and the most wonderful butterfly farm, where hundreds of butterflies and birds fly freely in a tropical environment, with luscious

hibiscus plants thriving at the edges of ponds and fountains filled with gleaming koi carp. The botanical gardens stretch over an area of around 2,000 sq m (21,527 sq ft).

4 Slottsruinen (The Royal Chateau)★

Often described as a ruin, Slottsruinen is actually rather impressive. It was Gustav III's dream to have his very own Versailles-style chateau, but after his assassination building work stopped, and today the palace remains just as it was left. The pale yellow façade of the building is sadly all that you will see, as it is not open to the public.

5 Gustav III's Paviljong★★★
☎ 08 402 61 30
Open 15 May-31 Aug. Tue.-Sun. noon-3pm; Sept. Sat.-Sun. noon-3pm. (guided tours only). Entrance charge.

Whilst awaiting completion of his chateau, Gustav III commissioned this pavilion, with plans drafted by Olof Tempelman and interior designed by Louis Masreliez. Don't miss the library, with its

leather-bound tomes carrying the Haga seal, and the lovely 'mirror room' with windows overlooking the water.

6 Ekotemplet★
7 Kinesiska Pagoden★

These two small, typically 18th-century style edifices stand in the park – the first an open-air dining room for the king, the second a Chinese pagoda. The pagoda is simple in style and a good example of the Oriental taste at the time.

8 Haga Forum★★
Annerovägen, 4
☎ 08 33 48 44
Open Mon.-Sat. 11.30am-midnight (last orders 10pm), Sun 11.30am-6pm.

This trendy restaurant is located in a former bus terminal, now used as a conference centre. Lunch is pricey, so you might prefer to settle for a beer out on the terrace opposite the pontoons. If it's chilly, you can sit inside by the fire and admire the 1960s James Bond-style decor.

Drottningholm, the royal palace

Just an hour away from the city centre, Drottningholm has been the home of the Swedish royal family since 1981. This quiet paradise by the water is a much more attractive royal home than the austere Kungliga Slottet located in the busy shopping area of Gamla Stan. Drottningholm is set in the midst of a lovely garden and huge park, but don't expect to see any of the royal family here, as they are well protected from the public gaze.

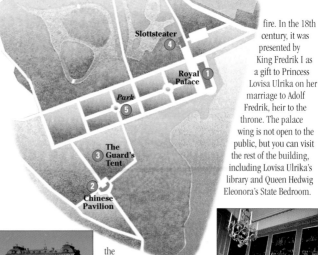

fire. In the 18th century, it was presented by King Fredrik I as a gift to Princess Lovisa Ulrika on her marriage to Adolf Fredrik, heir to the throne. The palace wing is not open to the public, but you can visit the rest of the building, including Lovisa Ulrika's library and Queen Hedwig Eleonora's State Bedroom.

❶ The Royal Palace★★

☎ 08 402 62 80
Open May-Aug. every day 10am-4.30pm; Sept. every day noon-3.30pm; Oct.-Apr. Sat.-Sun. noon-3.30pm. Entrance charge.

Drottningholm is one of the greatest works of two Swedish architects – Tessin the Elder, who began work on the palace in 1662, and his son Tessin the Younger, who completed it after his father's death. The palace has since been rebuilt a number of times, after being damaged by

❷ The Chinese Pavilion★★★

☎ 08 402 62 70
Open May-Aug. every day 11am-4.30pm, Sept. every day noon-3.30pm. Entrance charge.

The Chinese Pavilion, a Rococo gem, was given to Queen Lovisa Ulrika as a birthday gift by King Adolf Fredrik in 1753. Used as a royal summerhouse, it's brimming with treasures, including lacquered panels in the 'Red Room' and sumptuous embroidered murals. Nearby are a number of other pavilions – the dining room (the 'Confidence Room') and the former billiard room, which now houses a collection of tools.

GETTING TO DROTTNINGHOLM

Even if you're only in Stockholm for a few days, you should definitely try to visit Drottningholm. The most pleasurable way to arrive is by boat, and the *Drottningholm* and *Karl Filip* vessels leave daily, every hour from 10am (May–Sept., ☎ 08 46 85 87), from Klara Mälarstrand quay near the town hall. The journey takes an hour. Alternatively, you can take the metro to Brommaplan and then take any of the buses numbered 301-323 to the Drottningholm stop

❸ The Guard's Tent★
Open mid-June to mid-Aug. every day noon-4pm. Entrance free.

Along the path leading to the Chinese Pavilion you'll find a miniature version of one of the tents erected at the centre of Haga Park. Built out of painted metal in 1781, the tent was home to the royal guards. Inside you'll find a realistic reconstruction of the original interior.

❹ Slottsteater (Court Theatre)★★★
☎ 08 759 04 06
Open May, every day noon-4.30pm; June, 11am-4.30pm; Sept., 1-3.30pm. Guided tours only. Entrance charge.

This theatre dates from the 18th-century and is the oldest in Europe still to be operating

in its original design. It boasts papier-mâché stage decor, the original backdrops and hand-driven stage machinery, as well as a wonderful display of 18th-century special effects. The seating arrangement was very democratic, allowing royalty to rub shoulders with the general public, although a box was reserved for royal mistresses, who came to the shows incognito. Nearby, in Duke Carl's pavilion, a small theatre museum houses stage models and set designs from the 18th century, as well as an interesting gift shop.

❺ The Park★★★
The wonderful French-style Baroque gardens that back on to the palace are a real masterpiece. Paths lined with lime trees, yew tree topiary mazes and a pretty pond all add to the charm. Over 300 years old, the fragile gardens were restored between 1999 and 2001. Visitors are allowed to relax on the side lawns.

❻ Drottningholm Wärdshus★★
Malmbacken (on the opposite side of the road which runs alongside the palace).
☎ 08 759 03 08.

This establishment, originally built in the 19th century as a home for a rich widow, has been transformed many times over the years. In 1996 it was turned into a restaurant, retaining its low-ceilings rooms and an old-fashioned charm. Today it serves an excellent international cuisine and its sophisticated rustic appeal and inspired menu make it a perfect spot to relax and indulge yourself. There's also a lovely inner garden.

Rooms and restaurants
practicalities

HOTELS

Hotels in Stockholm are not as numerous as you might think. There are no formal categories (except for the really up-market, palacial establishments), and standards are very high, with almost all hotels offering a good level of comfort and cleanliness. The rooms are sometimes quite small and you may find you have a shower rather than a bath, but you're unlikely to come across any dingy hotels. The big chains, including Scandic and Radisson, are great value for money. The current trend is for hotels to be designed or refurbished by top Swedish designers.

BOOKING A ROOM

Stockholm is a popular venue for conferences, seminars and conventions, which means that hotels can often be very busy. Make sure you book your accommodation as soon as you decide to travel, or you may find there's a shortage of availability for the dates you want to stay. The Stockholm Information Service has a comprehensive listing of hotels (and youth hostels) in and around the city and you can request their brochure by contacting: Hotellcentralen, Centralstationen SE-111, Stockholm, ☎ +46 8 789 24 90 ❶ +46 8 791 86 66, email: hotels@stoinfo.se. They also have a website: www.stockholmtown.com

where you can choose which part of town and price range you want to go for. You can ask Hotellcentralen to book your room for you for a fee (taking advantage of last minute special offers), or reserve your accommodation directly with the hotel.

ROOM TARIFFS

All hotels offer special weekend deals which can be excellent value. You might well get a suite for the price of a standard double room. Some establishments hold these attractive prices for the month of July. On the other hand, prices don't change much (if at all) during the rest of the year, except for individual promotional offers or packages organised with SAS (Scandinavian Airlines) and the tourist office. A double room doesn't come cheap in Stockholm, on average costing between 1,000kr and 3,000kr, but for some reason, the top luxury hotels (with the exception of the Grand Hotel) are not that exorbitantly expensive in comparison, so you may feel you want to splash out!

RESTAURANTS

In recent years a few young, talented and well-travelled

Swedish chefs have revolutionised their country's cuisine, using fresh and simple ingredients and incorporating them into traditionally robust dishes, adding exotic flavours from distant climes. There are a few good Italian trattorias and a smattering of excellent Asian and Middle Eastern restaurants in Stockholm, but in general, good ethnic cuisine is thin on the ground. You're better off giving the new-style Swedish cooking a try.

THE SWEDISH WAY

The Swedes take breakfast very seriously. It consists of a selection of breads, charcuterie and cheese, together with pickled herrings, gherkins, dressed salads and a variety of pâtés. All these delicious delicacies are washed down with a cup of coffee. The Swedes also have their own unique way of dealing with beds. A double bed is made up of two adjacent mattresses with two separate duvets. The mattresses are then covered by a third, smaller mattress to ensure total comfort and an excellent night's sleep.

LOCAL CUSTOMS

Swedes tend to go to bed late but dine early. They have a light lunch between 11am and 1pm and eat dinner from 5pm onwards (rarely after 8pm except in a handful of restaurants). It's advisable to book a table for dinner through your hotel concierge. The Swedes are very ecologically aware and you'll find that the tap water is not only safe, but also has a pleasant taste, and is often served with strips of lemon rind and delivered to your table free of charge. If you order water, you will be brought a small bottle of fizzy mineral water (still mineral water is just plain tap water). You can order well-known brands such as Evian or Vittel but they will be expensive. Even though it may not be very warm in Stockholm, it doesn't stop the locals sitting outside. Every seat on a restaurant terrace or in an open-air café is provided with a colourful woollen blanket to keep you warm, but don't be tempted to walk off with it or you'll be in big trouble! Children are always welcome and can accompany their parents everywhere. From fast food outlets to trendy establishments, every restaurant is equipped with high chairs and a special menu for kids.

PRICES

Eating in Stockholm is not a cheap business. A starter costs around 100-150kr and a main course will set you back 180-200kr, but portions are huge and you can easily fill up on one dish. In Sweden, a three-course meal consisting of starter, main course and dessert is quite a gargantuan feast. At lunchtime, most locals enjoy a *caffe latte* and a pastry (a saffron or cinnamon bun, or a bagel with raw onion and soft cheese) in one of the many *konditori* chains, such as Wayne's Café, Coffe Cup or Tully's. If you want a real Italian coffee, pop into Sosta (Jakobergsgatan 5/7, ☎ 08 611 71 07, open Mon.-Fri. 8am-7pm, Sat. 10am-5pm). Some restaurants, cafés and soup bars have set menus at lunchtime (50-70kr), consisting of a savoury main course and a dessert, plus a cup of tea or coffee. Due to the strict alcohol regulations, wine prices are exorbitant and can more than double the bill. However, you can order by the glass, which like the portions tend to be rather generous in size, and keep the costs down. Service is included, but most people round up the bill by adding 10kr, 20kr or 30kr tops. If you pay by credit card you'll need to add the tip to the slip before signing.

FINDING YOUR WAY AROUND

Each entry in the Rooms and Restaurants, Shopping and Nightlife sections of this guide is accompanied by a grid reference, which refers to its location on the general map on pages 138-139.

HOTELS

Vasastaden

Birger Jarl★★★

Tulegatan, 8 (C1)
☎ 08 674 18 00
☏ 08 673 73 66
www.birgerjarl.se
Double room 1,835kr;
suite 2,650kr (weekend
rates available).

This ultra-modern hotel is
excellent value for money, given
the delights on offer. Housed in
a somewhat charmless 1960s
building, its new director, Yvonne
Sörensen, has given it a fresh
lease of life. She commissioned
the talented and fashionable
Swedish duo Thomas Sandell
and Jonas Bohlin to give the
rooms and suites a new look.
Exhibitions are held in the lobby
and special 'design weekends'
are offered, with entry to
museums and reductions in
some shops included. The staff
are very friendly and efficient.

Lydmar

of the city, between Stureplan
and Hummlegården. The rooms
are very comfortable and the
service impeccable, but apart
from its piano bar, the hotel lacks
real warmth and charm.

Lydmar★★★

Sturegatan, 10 (D1-2)
☎ 08 56 61 13 00
☏ 08 56 61 13 01
www.lydmar.se
Double rooms: medium
2,300kr; Large 2,550kr;
extra large 3,850kr;

Birger Jarl

Stureplan

Scandic Anglais★★

Humlegårdsgatan, 23 (D2)
☎ 08 517 340 00
☏ 08 517 340 11
www.scandic-hotels.se
Double room around
1,963kr (depending on
season and special offers).

The best thing about this hotel
is its location, right in the heart

newly refurbished suite
with garden view: 4,950kr
(weekend rates available).

This hotel has been refurbished
in 1970s style and is the trendiest spot in town. The reception
area is in the middle of the lobby-
cum-bar, a popular rendezvous
point in the evenings. If you feel
like a special treat, book the new
suite (which is as big as an

entire loft) on the top floor – the
view across the garden of the
Royal Library is really quite
something.

Östermalm

Diplomat★★★

Strandvägen, 7C (D2/E2)
☎ 08 459 68 00
☏ 08 459 68 20
www.srs-worldhotels.com
Double room 1,795kr;
luxury double 1,895kr
(weekend rates available).

This is one of the most chic
hotels in Stockholm, but not the
most expensive. Take advantage
of the special weekend rates. The
Art Nouveau building dates
from 1911 and it has a wonderful view over Nybrovicken. The
stark contrast between the
classical rooms and ultra-
modern restaurant-bar is quite
stunning.

Esplanade★★

Strandvägen, 7A (D2/E2)
☎ 08 663 07 40
🖷 08 662 59 92
www.hotelesplanade.se
Double room 2,295kr;
weekend rate 1,695kr.

More discreet than the Diplomat, its neighbour and sister hotel, this family hotel has 32 rooms, all furnished in Swedish Art Nouveau style. It has a certain old-fashioned charm and a slightly nostalgic atmosphere, but its sea view and excellent value for money make it a good place to stay.

Pärlan★★★

Skeppargatan, 27 (D1-2)
☎ 08 663 50 70
🖷 08 667 71 45
Double room: 950kr
(weekend rates available)

Just minutes away from Östermalmstorget, this tiny hotel has only 8 rooms and is housed in an apartment built in the early 20th century. There are many reasons to stay here, including the friendly, family atmosphere, the lovely warm dining room heated by a stove, the good food and the Chesterfield sofas. It's also great value for money.

Blasieholmen

Berns★★★

Näckströmsgatan, 8 (D2)
☎ 08 566 320 00
🖷 08 566 322 01
www.berns.se
Double rooms from 2,500kr;
suites from 4.250kr
(weekend rates available).

Located in the city centre, but away from the hustle and bustle, this hotel has 65 rooms that combine luxury with taste. The bar and restaurant, designed by Sir Terence Conran, have gilding, chandeliers and elaborate ceilings. The rooms are less original in decor – although there's a lovely suite in the tower with a bull's eye window housing the exterior clock – but the Art Nouveau building is magnificent in itself. The private sauna is an added incentive.

Grand Hotel★★★★

Blasieholmshammen, 8 (D2)
☎ 08 679 35 00
🖷 08 611 86 86
Double rooms from 3,200kr;
Nobel Suite 11,000kr
(weekend rates available).

The Grand Hotel's wonderful Art Nouveau façade overlooks the royal palace, on the edge of Norrström. It's a legendary hotel

in which the winners of the Nobel Prize and their families stay during the ceremony. Dari Fo, winner of the 1997 Nobel Prize for Literature, enjoyed the hospitality of this very refined hotel, with an entourage of no less than 20 people. The hotel's top restaurant, 'Franska Matsalen', is a must for gourmets, and the 'Veranden' is a great place for a *smörgåsbord*. The Grand also offers a range of special packages, including 'You deserve the Best', which allows you to stay in the hotel for only 795kr per person per night.

Radisson SAS Strand★★

Nybrokajen, 9 (D2)
☎ 08 50 66 40 00
🖷 08 50 66 40 01
www.radisson.com
Double rooms 2,300-3,500kr (weekend rates 1,595-1,900kr).

This classic hotel has a perfect location, set on the edge of Nybroviken. The rooms have a chic, sophisticated style, with a modern Gustavian flavour, and are very comfortable. Some of them also boast beautiful sea views. The dining room is designed like an Italian piazza and is quite amazing.

Långholmen

STF Vandrarhem, IYHF Youth Hostel

Kronohäktet,
Långholmen (B3)
☎ 08 66 80 510
🖷 08 72 08 575
Double 'cell' 995kr.

On the island of Långholmen, Stockholm's most up-market STF youth hostel is housed in the former prison building (1724). The cells have been converted into smart dormitory rooms.

It has a good location and views, and you can even visit the small prison museum (open every day 11am-4pm).

Norrmalm

Nordic See and Nordic Light★★

Vasaplan (C2)
☎ 08 505 630 00
🖷 08 505 630 60
Double rooms from 2,400kr; extra large double room 3,400kr (weekend rates available).

These two hotels are the newest in Stockholm and among the most trendy. They are located close to the departure point for the Arlanda Express, which runs between the city centre and the airport. As their names suggest, the decor centres on the sea and light, respectively. Inside, design is king, but the atmosphere is a little cold and all the rooms follow the same theme. The lobby of the Nordic Light, however, is wonderful. This is really a spot for those who go more for design than ambience.

Södermalm

Hotell Anno 1647★★★

Mariagränd, 3 (D3)
☎ 08 442 16 80
🖷 08 442 16 47
Double room 1,795kr; suite 2,995kr (weekend rates available).

This 17th-century building is full of charm. The rooms have pine floors and period furniture, and are decorated in a rustic style. In sharp contrast, the breakfast room and bar on the ground floor have been refurbished in a very trendy, ultra-modern style. It's well-placed for the Old Town.

Scandic Sjöfartshotellet★★

Katarinavägen, 26 (D3)
☎ 08 517 349 00
🖷 08 517 349 11
www.scandic-hotels.com
Standard double room from around 1,500kr.

This Scandic hotel, close to the Katarina Hissen lift and ideally located near Söder and the Old

Hotell Anno 1647

Town, isn't trendy or chic, but it's a good place to stay with children. The rooms are very comfortable and resemble ocean-liner cabins. It's good value for money and the staff are very friendly.

Gamla Stan

Lady Hamilton★★

Storkyrkobrinken, 5 (C3/D3)
☎ 08 506 401 00
🅕 08 506 401 10
www.victory-hotel.se
Double rooms from 2,350kr; weekend rates from 1,650kr.

This traditional, attractive hotel, housed in a 15th-century building, is both Swedish and British in style. It has a lovely atmosphere that makes you feel as if you've stepped back in time. A wooden figurehead in the form of Lady Hamilton welcomes guests into the entrance hall, which is decorated with statues and paintings with a maritime theme. The rooms are furnished in Swedish rustic style with antique furniture and are named after flowers.

Lord Nelson★★

Västerlånggatan, 22 (D3)
☎ 08 506 401 20
🅕 08 506 401 30
www.victory-hotel.se
Double rooms from 1,990kr; weekend rates from 1,350kr.

Lord Nelson, whose mistress was of course Lady Hamilton, gave his name to this charming hotel, housed in a Jugendstil building that looks rather like a ship. The nautical theme continues on the roof terrace, from where there's a fine view over the town hall steeple. Each floor is named after a different deck of a ship (e.g. poop deck).

Victory★★

Lilla Nygatan, 5 (C3/D3)
☎ 08 506 400 00
🅕 08 506 400 10
www.victory-hotel.se
Double rooms from 2,490kr; suites from 3,890kr; weekend rates from 1,790kr.

In 1937, the owner of this building, a potato merchant called Andersson, discovered a treasure chest of silver coins in his cellar. They are now displayed in the Royal Coin Cabinet (Slottsbacken, 6, ☎ 08 519 553

04, open daily 10am-4pm). If you treat yourself to the large suite, take a close look at the ceiling, painted back in 1640.

Hotel J★★★

Ellensviksvägen, 1 (off map)
☎ 08 601 30 00
🅕 08 601 30 09
www.hotelj.com
Double rooms 1,595-3,395kr (weekend rates available).

This chic and discreet hotel, standing in a pretty garden at the water's edge, between the city and the archipelago, is a real haven of peace and tranquillity. The rooms have a nautical theme, with pale wooden furniture, striped fabrics and photos of the America's Cup. The breakfast room is very attractive.

Stallmästare-gården★★★

Norrtull, 113 (B1)
☎ 08 610 13 00
🅕 08 610 13 40
www.stallmastaregarden.se
Double rooms from 2,400kr; weekend rate 1,300kr.

Built around the oldest inn in Stockholm (early 17th century), this new hotel combines the modern and the traditional. It was constructed in sympathy with the original architecture, and the rooms are decorated in a contemporary Asian style. It's an ideally located, perfect retreat.

Hotel J, Nacka Strand

RESTAURANTS

Norrmalm

Fredsgatan, 12★★★

Fredsgatan, 12 (C2)
☎ 08 24 80 52
Closed July.

Danyel Couet is a young Franco-Swedish restaurateur with considerable gastronomic flair. His inventive cuisine has earned him a coveted star in the French *Michelin Guide Rouge* as well as many accolades in the Swedish press. Together with chef Melker Andersson, he offers a delicious combination of Swedish and international cuisine, mixing the traditional with a hint of the exotic. His unique style of 'fusion food' is served up in a classical/modern dining room that is regularly refurbished. Housed in the Academy of Fine Arts building, the restaurant has a lovely view of Lake Mälaren and the Old Town. This popular and trendy meeting place becomes a lively disco in the summer months.

Halv Trappa Plus Gård★★

Lästmakargatan, 3 (C2)
Metro Östermalstorg
☎ 08 611 02 76
Open for dinner only, 6-11pm.

This bar-restaurant is one of the city's most popular venues. Descending the three steps down to the dining room, you enter a warm, intimate space, with fabric-covered walls and soft lighting, where you can enjoy a unique global cuisine. A spiral staircase leads to a mezzanine courtyard, surrounded by buildings. The atmosphere is very lively during summer weekends.

Divino★★★

Karlavägen, 28 (C1/D1-2/E2)
☎ 08 611 02 69.

Although the embassy district is rather quiet, this top Italian restaurant is worth the detour. It's a mix of white walls and beige-coloured linen, and the young chef, Jodi Cohen, prepares wonderfully sophisticated dishes from Tuscany, Lombardy and Piedmont. There's an impressive list of Italian wines, all available by the glass, as well as a large selection of *grappa*.

Rolf Kök★★★

Tegnérgatan, 41 (C1/2)
☎ 08 10 16 96
Open weekdays 11am-1am,
Sat.-Sun. 5pm-1am.

This is one of the most trendy places to eat in the city, serving a menu of modern Swedish cuisine (with wonderful fish) in

an original setting designed by Jonas Bohlin and Thomas Sandell. The star duo have added a hint of irony to their design, with chairs fixed to the concrete walls, high tables and bar stools, plus a surprise in the bathrooms – two loos positioned next to each other for couples who just can't bear to be separated even for a moment!

East★★

Stureplan, 13 (D2)
☎ 08 611 49 59.

Delicious Asian-style stir-fried food is served in this popular and trendy (with a capital 'T') restaurant. If you just want a drink, however, make for the bar, which stays open late.

City

Restaurangen★★★

Oxtorgsgatan, 14 (C2)
☎ 08 22 09 52
Open Mon.-Sat. 11am-1am
(closed July).

The atmosphere here is lively, relaxed and youthful and the interior very attractive. You can watch all the food being cooked in the open kitchen (an original idea from top chef Danyel Couet). Meals are not made up of the traditional trilogy of starter, main course and dessert,

but are put together according to flavours, such as saffron, coriander, garlic, chocolate etc., served in three or five small dishes. At lunchtime, the meals are created in advance airline-style, but with far more up-market and delicious results!

Grodan Sergel★

Hitechbuilding
Sveavägen, 9 (C1-2)
☎ 08 50 67 83 00
Grev Turegatan, 16
☎ 08 679 61 00.

With outlets in both the centre and the City, the 'Frog Bistro' (the motif appears everywhere) is the perfect spot to enjoy a quick lunch, club sandwich or aperitif. The latter is particularly popular with those who work in the Hitechbuilding, as the bistro is situated at the foot of the tower.

Östermalm

PA & Co★★★

Riddargatan, 8 (D2)
Metro Östermalstorg
☎ 08 611 08 45
Open for dinner only
(open Sun.).

This tiny restaurant was hailed the crucible of modern Swedish cuisine. Journalists, artists and advertising executives gather here to enjoy the warm, relaxed atmosphere and excellent food. Arrive early or you may miss out, as you can't book in advance. The menu includes well-cooked meat dishes, such as reindeer and centres around fresh Swedish produce. The wine list is also very impressive, including examples of vintages from Francis Ford Coppola's vineyards.

Teatergrillen★★★

Nybrogatan, 3 (D2)
☎ 08 679 68 42
Open Mon.-Fri. 11.30am-2.30pm, 5pm-midnight, Sat. 5pm-midnight.

Teatergrillen, the sister restaurant of PA & Co, has recently had a complete makeover by the great Jonas Bohlin. Head for the bar and sample the traditional *smörrebröd*, open sandwiches topped with salmon, liver pâté or potato salad and served on Danish black rye bread. The atmosphere is great and the interior very attractive. The perfect solution for late night hunger pangs.

Pascha★★★

Grevgatan, 9 (D2)
Metro Östermalstorg
☎ 08 660 63 93
Open for dinner only,
closed Sun.

With an Oriental-style decor
including low tables, divans
and subtle lighting, this small
restaurant boasts a very trendy
and chic clientele. The two
owners, Paul and Emilio, one of
Armenian descent and the other
Italian, are local celebrities that
are regularly seen on the pages
of people-spotting magazines.
The Lebanese food is delicious,
particularly the succulent grilled
lamb.

Riche★★★

Birger Jarlsgatan, 4
(C1-2/D2)
☎ 08 679 68 40
Open Mon.-Fri. 11.30am-
2am, Sat. 1pm-2am.

The PA & Co team has recently
taken over the reins of this
much-loved, hundred-year-old
institution, and inside a quiet
revolution is taking place. The
traditional cuisine is undergo-
ing subtle modernisation by the

dynamic chefs, while the decor
has been brought into the 21st
century by the skilful hands of
Jonas Bohlin. The atmosphere is
lively and friendly and the food
excellent. It's also one of the few
restaurants in Stockholm where
you can dine late.

Ett Litet Hak★

Grev Turegatan, 13-15
(D1-2)
Metro Östermalstorg
☎ 08 660 13 09.

Strategically located on the main
artery for shopaholics, this small
restaurant makes a good spot for
a quick lunch during a hectic
shopping trip. You can enjoy
a generous salad, a plate of
steamed fish or a glass of wine
with a selection of dishes. The
dining room has grey walls and
pale wooden tables and the
terrace overlooks the pedestrian-
ised street.

Il Conte★★

Grevgatan, 9 (D2)
☎ 08 661 26 28
Open for dinner only.

Sheltered from the busy shopping streets in the centre (just a

few minutes away on foot), this
pretty Italian restaurant with its
red walls, serves a delicious range
of pasta dishes and a variety of
Transalpine specialities, all very
authentic since the owner was
born in Italy.

Sturehof★★★

Stureplan, at the entrance
to the Sturegallerian (D2)
☎ 08 679 87 50
Last orders 1am.

If you prefer to eat late, you'll
adore this lovely brasserie, which
is immensely popular with the
locals. Here once again you can
see the talented work of Jonas

Bohlin, who has successfully revamped the place, combining tradition with the very latest in modern design. The inhabitants of Stockholm love it, which means it's usually very busy. However, you can always enjoy a glass of wine at one of the two bars while you're waiting for a table. It's quite pricey but the atmosphere and innovative decor make it all worthwhile.

Kungsträdgården

The Opera House, built in 1787, is home to a first class restaurant complex, comprising the main dining room, Café Opera, Opera Bar and the 'Hip Pocket'. Open every day (except mid-July to mid-August), they have become some of Stockholm's most popular late night venues, earning international as well as local reputations and catering to all tastes.

Operakällaren★★★
Operan
Karl XII Torget (D2)
☎ 08 676 58 10
Open every day 6-10pm.

This stunning restaurant offers you the chance to dine in splendour alongside members of Stockholm's chic society. Its sumptuous early 20th-century decor includes a coffered ceiling, oak panelling, Art Nouveau

Café Opera

paintings and copper lights. The dress code is smart, but if you forget to wear a tie, you can always borrow one from the staff. The Italian master chef, Stefano Catenacci, prepares a wonderful gastronomic cuisine and the wine list, selected by the French director, Jean-Paul Bénèzeth, is just as impressive. The service is impeccable and attentive, the atmosphere delightful and the view incomparable. All in all, it's a perfect place to enjoy a few moments of luxury.

Café Opera★★★
Operan
Karl XII Torget (D2)
☎ 08 676 58 07
Open every day 5pm-3am.

This venue is just as wonderful as the main dining room, but the atmosphere is more relaxed and the clientele generally more youthful. It's also not quite as expensive as the Operakällaren. Young royals and chic diners have been coming here for years and its international reputation is well deserved. The beautiful Art Nouveau decor is an experience not to be missed, and you can enjoy the liberty of dining here until 1 o'clock in the morning. At night the Café Opera also doubles as a night-club and casino.

Backfickan★★
Operan
Karl XII Torget (D2)
☎ 08 676 58 09
Open Mon.-Fri. 11am-11.30pm, Sat. noon-11.30pm, closed Sunday.

The 'Hip Pocket' (located at the back of the opera house), has been serving delicious food for over 40 years. It's well loved by locals, who enjoy its relaxed and warm atmosphere. The walls are covered with portraits of artists and the U-shaped bar can only accommodate 30 people. The tasty, traditional Swedish food is cheaper than in other venues in Kungsträdgården.

Blasieholmen

Berns Restaurang, Bar & Grill★★

Näckströmsgatan, 8 (D2)
Berzelii Park
☎ 08 566 322 22.

Housed in the luxury Berns hotel, this restaurant and bar, located near Berzelii park, are compulsory stops on your nocturnal itinerary. Since Sir Terence Conran redesigned the interior, this has become one of the smartest brasseries in town. It has a beautiful ceiling with crystal chandeliers, a well-lit bar and extra deep and comfy chairs. The upstairs veranda is more relaxed, particularly when the windows are open in summer. Strindberg is said to have picked up ideas here for his novel, *The Red Room* (*Röda Rummet*).

Gamla Stan

Pontus in the Green House★★★

Österlånggatan, 17 (D3)
Metro Gamla Stan
or bus no. 46
☎ 08 23 85 00
Lunch 11.30am-3pm;
dinner 6-11pm, closed Sun.

This elegant restaurant, housed in a building dating back to the 18th century, is one of the city's most popular spots. The young chef, Pontus Frithiof, the first Scandinavian to have been awarded a star by the *Michelin Guide Rouge*, serves luxury food inspired by the legendary French chef Escoffier, but with a distinctly contemporary touch. Pontus in the Green House offers two options – a set dish plus a glass of wine served in a cosy atmosphere, or dinner served upstairs in the more traditional, formal dining room. If you're feeling tempted to indulge in some gourmet delicacies, then this is certainly the place to do it, but it's not cheap. You can also enjoy sushi at the bar or sample some of the caviar.

Bistro Ruby and Grill Ruby★

Österlånggatan, 14 (D3)
☎ 08 20 60 15
Open every day 5pm-1am
(Grill Ruby), 5-11pm
(Bistro Ruby).

Bistro Ruby is a traditional bistro serving French-style food. The owner, Mikael Malmberg, loves Beaujolais and offers an excellent wine list, including a large selection of French bottles.

Grill Ruby, just next door, serves American-style grills and weekend brunches. The atmosphere is less formal and it's one of the few places in the old part of town which isn't full of tourists.

Den Gyldene Freden★

Österlånggatan, 51 (D3)
☎ 02 24 97 60
Closed July.

'The Golden Peace' is Stockholm's oldest restaurant, having

Pelikan

first opened its doors in 1772. Its walls are covered in the words of the 18th-century Swedish poet, Bellman. Today, the Academy of Letters, responsible for awarding the annual Nobel Prize for Literature, dines here every week in a private dining room. The atmosphere, style and cuisine are unique, but so are the prices (around 350kr for two courses).

Södermalm

Pelikan★★★

Blekingegatan, 40 (C4/D4)
☎ **08 743 06 95**
Open for dinner only.

This wonderful old beer hall is full of atmosphere and attracts some real characters. In the 1960s, the Pelikan (first established in the 17th century and housed in a variety of locations during its life), finally settled in this beautiful early 20th-century building. Its Jugendstil decor and ceiling frescoes have been preserved intact. The food is traditional and the place is popular with local musicians, artists and actors, who enjoy the lively atmosphere.

Gondolen★★★

Stadsgårdsleden, 6 (D3)
☎ **08 641 70 90**
Open Mon.-Fri. 11.30am-1am, Sat. 1pm-1am

If you don't mind heights and are looking for somewhere special to eat with a wonderful view and fabulous food, then Gondolen is the perfect answer. The restaurant is situated on the

top floor of the Katarina Hissen lift, just above Slussen, and commands a fantastic view over the city. The food is just as stunning, with delicious fish and meat dishes, such as gravadlax with asparagus and roasted reindeer fillet, all prepared by a top chef in a relaxed atmosphere.

FBK Folkoperan Bar & Kök★★

Hornsgatan, 72 (B3/C3)
☎ **08 616 07 42**
Open every day noon-1am.

FBK is worth a visit even if it's only for a glass of something. The atmosphere is great and it's usually full of performers who pop in for a drink after the show. The somewhat original decor includes a mural-covered staircase sporting geometric designs in black and white. The restaurant serves a range of traditional Swedish dishes, and the barman certainly knows his stuff.

Shopping practicalities

If you're a fan of international designer labels, including Swedish examples, then head for the city centre and take a wander around Stureplan, Östermalm and Hötorget. Those who prefer the latest look or vintage clothes should make a beeline for Södermalm.

WHERE TO GO SHOPPING

The quality shops in Stockholm are concentrated around a few streets in Östermalm and Norrmalm, starting with the very chic Birger Jarlsgatan, lined with luxury stores selling more or less the same clothes as you'll find in any other major capital city. The adjacent streets have a more Swedish feel – Nybrogatan, Grev Turegatan, Biblioteksgatan, Mäster Samuelsgatan and Jakobsbergsgatan. The famous Sturegallerian is the nerve centre of Swedish shopping, but the Norrmalm district – Kungsgatan, Hamngatan, Hötorget and Drottninggatan – has all the big national stores, including the legendary H&M.

Living up to its bohemian image, Södermalm is home to the more arty shops, with secondhand and handcrafted items available in Hornsgatan. Other interesting shops worth exploring can be found along Götgatan, Nytorgsgatan, Asögatan and Bondegatan.

Although there are a few antique shops worth visiting in Gamla Stan, there are also an overwhelming number of touristy souvenir outlets, selling items that are sometimes of rather dubious taste.

FINDING YOUR WAY AROUND

Each entry in the Rooms and Restaurants, Shopping and Nightlife sections of this guide is accompanied by a grid reference, which refers to its location on the general map on pages 138-139.

OPENING HOURS

Strangely enough, Saturday – the traditional day for shopping – is the day when the shops close early.

SALES

On the first day of the sales the shops are so full that you may decide you can't face the hassle. However, there are often some fabulous deals to be had and braving the crowds is usually worth the effort. Reductions of 30-40% are normal (and sometimes even up to 50%) on the first days of the sale. The summer sales start on the Monday after the St John festival weekend (around 21st of June) and last until the end of August. In winter they start after Christmas and last until early February.

In the centre, shops, along with cafés and *konditori*, are open continuously from 10am to 6pm, Monday to Friday and from 11am to 4pm on Saturday. The larger shops and clothing chain stores in Hamngatan stay open until 7pm during the week and are open on Sunday from noon to 4pm. In Gamla Stan the hours are less reliable and many shops don't open their doors until noon during the week and are firmly closed at the weekend. Other more touristy venues are open on Sunday. The shops in Söder also operate rather flexible hours, often opening at 11am and closing at 6pm weekdays (4pm on Saturday), but are closed on Sunday.

HOW TO PAY

If you don't fancy walking around with your pockets full of cash, you can always pay with a credit card, even for the smallest amounts (although it is worth checking first) and in the smallest outlets. Most places accept the major cards (American Express, Visa, Diner's Club, Eurocard) – but if you're not sure, take a look at the stickers on the door or window. Then all you have to do is sign the slip. You can only cash travellers' cheques in banks, so the rates are not always to your advantage, but you can withdraw money direct from cash machines at any time of the day or night.

CUSTOMS REGULATIONS

Sadly, tax refunds don't apply to EU residents. If you're visiting friends in Stockholm, don't forget that importing cigarettes and alcohol is strictly regulated (see p. 7). There is no limit to the amount of goods EU citizens can bring back from Sweden, as long as they are for personal use. HM Customs & Excise provides the following guidelines for what they deem acceptable limits: 10 litres of spirits, 90 litres of wine, 110 litres of beer, 3,200 cigarettes, 200 cigars, 400 cigarillos and 3kg leaf tobacco.

CLOTHES SIZES

While hunting for the perfect outfit, don't forget that clothes sizes in Sweden may differ from those at home. Most sales assistants should be able to help you find the perfect fit, but we have compiled size conversion tables (see p. 140) for easy reference.

SHIPPING YOUR GOODS HOME

If you buy large goods whilst you're in Stockholm, the shop can arrange to have them shipped back home. The large department stores (NK and Åhléns) will also do this for you, but in both cases, the cost of the transport will be added to your bill.

WOMEN'S FASHION

Stockholm is a city for the young and is focusing its sights more and more on the world of fashion, in particular chic, expensive, designer gear. It's still slightly behind other European cities, but local manufacture is on the increase, mainly in the area of cool, trendy designs seen on the world's catwalks. At times you may feel you're wandering through the pages of *Wallpaper* magazine. Fashion is concentrated in the busy commercial streets of the city centre and around the main axis of Södermalm and Götgatan. The only disappointment is that there are very few stores selling shoes and accessories.

100% SWEDISH

H&M

Hamngatan, 22 & 14 (C2/D2)
Metro Centralen
☎ 08 79 65 434
or 08 79 65 489
Open Mon.-Fri. 10am-7pm,
Sat. 10am-5pm, Sun. noon-
4pm.

The famous H&M prêt-à-porter store has seven outlets in the city centre, but these two branches in Hamngatan are much larger and also open on Sunday. The collections are the same as in their other stores throughout Europe, but there are also a few exclusive designs. H&M reinterprets designs from the top international labels and produces simpler and cheaper high street versions. Bring your credit card along as it's difficult to resist the great collection of clothes, accessories, jewellery and underwear on sale here.

Filippa K

Grev Turegatan, 18 (D1-2)
Metro Östermalmstorg
☎ 08 545 888 88
Open Mon.-Fri. 10am-6pm,
Sat. 10am-4pm.

Filippa K is Sweden's best-known female designer, and her shop is a showcase of top-selling success stories. There are outlets in the city centre and in Södermalm (Götgatan, 23), as well as concessions in NK and Åhléns. Her designs are fresh, colourful and simple, with a youthful (but not excessively youthful) touch – but beware, they are a bit pricey.

Lars Wallin and Lisen Stibeck

Sibyllegatan, 19 (D1-2)
Metro Östermalmstorg
☎ 08 545 69 650
Open Mon.-Fri. 10am-6pm,
Sat. 10am-4pm.

This shop is more boudoir than boutique. People come here in search of an outfit for a special occasion or even the perfect dress

for the 'big day'. On the ground floor you'll find original jewellery in gold and semi-precious stones by Lisen Stibeck, alongside Lars Wallin's ready-to-wear range. The basement houses Wallin's studio and the fitting room for the made-to-measure outfits he creates in fabulous fabrics. An Asian-style, red-lacquered champagne bar completes this unique experience.

Björn Borg Clothing
Sergelgatan, 12-14 (C2)
Metro Centralen
☎ **08 217 040**
Open Mon.-Fri. 10am-6pm,
Sat. 11am-4pm.

The renowned tennis star has reinvented himself with his own collection of fashion clothing, launched with a range of youthful underwear in sporty, practical, but attractive styles. His swimwear and casual clothes are well cut and stylish. There are several of his stores in the city centre, as well as concessions in the larger department stores. The prices of his leisure clothes and accessories such as footwear, bags and belts are affordable, but watch out for the underwear and swimwear as they tend to be rather more expensive.

Anna Holtblad
Grev Turegatan, 13 (D1-2)
Metro Östermalmstorg
☎ **08 545 02 220**
Open Mon.-Fri. 10am-6pm,
Sat. 10am-4pm.

Anna Holtblad is another Swedish designer who has made a name for herself with an unpretentious but stylish range of clothes. She is best known for her multicoloured knitwear, made out of beautiful wool and fabrics. Her cardigans, sweaters, tops, socks and stockings are a delight.

Maria Westerlind
Drottninggatan, 81A
Metro Hötorget or
Rådmansgatan (C2)
☎ **08 23 45 45**
Open Mon.-Fri. 10am-6pm,
Sat. 10am-4pm.

This shop, with its pale grey walls and grey stone floor, provides a stylish, neutral backdrop to Maria Westerlind's fresh and colourful collection. She designs clothes, bags and accessories which can be

tried on behind the pretty checked curtains in the changing rooms. Since the company manufactures all its own products, they are generally good value for money.

YOUNG AND TRENDY

Whyred

Grev Turegatan, 26 (D1-2)
Metro Östermalmstorg
☎ **08 5280 0590**
Open Mon.-Fri. 10am-6pm, Sat. 10am-4pm.

Launched in 1998, this label (the creation of three young designers) opened its first shop in the spring of 2001. Here you'll find their collections as well as those of other young Scandinavian designers displayed in an avant-garde setting. Their leisure range is chic, simple, but different – denim jogging pants and leather or satin tops bring a certain elegance to the business of sport. Their mission is to mix styles rather than to create a total look. There's also a men's collection.

Design Torget Mode

Jakobsbergsgatan, 6 (C2)
Metro Östermalm-storg
☎ **08 440 32 80**
Open Mon.-Fri. 10am-6.30pm, Sat. 10am-4pm.

This is the kingdom of Scandinavian designers, operating as a community in which each designer rents a space to display their work. If you're looking for something new, different and a little avant-garde, the clothes and accessories should be right up your street and within your budget.

Jus

Birger Jarlsgatan, 22 (C1-2)
Metro Östermalmstorg
☎ **08 611 98 00**
Open Mon.-Fri. 10am-6pm, Sat. 10am-4pm.

There's a rather club-like atmosphere in this huge boutique, with its loud, pumping music and trendy gear. Ulrika Nilsson has created the perfect backdrop for a wide range of streetwear, Swedish jeans (Whyred, Burfitt) and international labels, such as Levi's Red. You'll also find creative designs here from Xuly Bët alongside

the experimental work of new and upcoming stylists. And if that isn't enough, upstairs there's a selection of the latest CDs and some pretty candles.

DESIGNER CHIC

Mrs H

Drottninggatan, 110 (C2)
Metro Rådmansgatan
☎ **08 30 01 02**
Open Mon.-Fri. 11am-6.30pm, Sat. 11am-4pm.

Against an all-white backdrop, Helene Andersson displays her relatively small, but extremely exclusive collection of top international designer clothes. Among them are such illustrious names as Paule Ka, Bruno Frisoni and Eric Bergère from France and the London designer duo Eley Kishimoto. Jade Jagger's jewellery collection and a sumptuous range of Scottish knitwear from the Cashmere Studio stand alongside Olivia Morris's exotic boots and Ole Henriksen's range of cosmetics. A must for all fashion victims.

Paul & Friends

Grev Turegatan, 7 (D1-2)
Metro Östermalmstorg
☎ 08 54 50 26 50
Open Mon.-Fri. 10am-6pm, Sat. 10am-4pm.

Paul & Friends is the place to come for all the latest designs. Here you'll find top international labels such as Prada, Miu Miu, Helmut Lang, Fendi, Comme des Garçons, Gaspard Yurkiewich and Pucci, as well as the house collection of simple and trendy designs. You may find that the big names are more

expensive than at home, so it's probably best to focus on Paul's own creations.

Paul & Friends Shoes

Birger Jarlsgatan, on corner with Biblioteksgatan (D2)
Metro Östermalmstorg
☎ 08 54 50 26 25
Open Mon.-Fri. 10am-6pm, Sat. 10am-4pm.

The same name, but this branch specialises in shoes and accessories from all over the world. Prada, Miu Miu, Marc Jacobs – they're all here, along with unusual designs by Jimmy Choo, Ernest Esposito and Premiata. Ask the sales team to help you choose and don't be put off by their glamorous appearance, it's all part of the experience.

Nathalie Schuterman

Grev Turegatan, 1 (D1-2)
Metro Östermalmstorg
☎ 08 611 62 01
Open Mon.-Fri. 10am-6pm, Sat. 10am-4pm.

MIA

Wollmar Yxkullsgatan, 8 (C3)
☎ 08 644 91 11
Open Mon.-Fri. noon-7pm.

Mia is Finnish and doesn't speak a word of English. She has a huge collection of secondhand clothes from the 1950s and 1960s, as well as jewellery and accessories, all displayed against the striking pink background of the shop. Have a good rummage and you may well find designer items at very attractive prices.

Another all-white boutique, filled with the latest rhythms and sounds, together with Nathalie Schuterman's ultra-chic international selection of clothes and shoes by Marc Jacobs, Marni, Michael Kors, Elspeth Gibson, Clements Ribeiro, Jimmy Choo and Emma Hope. It's a lovely spot, very friendly and welcoming and full of the latest designs.

MEN'S FASHION

In Sweden, labels exclusively for men are relatively rare. On the other hand, successful Swedish designers who launched their careers with collections for women have often followed them up with menswear ranges. They have concessions in the large stores, including NK and Åhléns, and in the attractive boutiques in the city centre. The designs are equally inventive and original, and Swedish men are just as stylishly attired as their female counterparts, taking inspiration from the trendiest fashion magazines.

Bondelid

Götgatan, 40 (D3-4)
Metro Medbordgarplatsen
☎ **08 462 00 68**
Open Mon.-Fri. 10am-6.30pm, Sat. 10am-4pm, Sun. noon-4pm.

This large store in Södermalm is the place to come for stylish, unpretentious, casual clothes with a hint of the 1950s about them. It's a sort of Swedish Gap, selling items in matching colours with a traditional cut.

Filippa K

Grev Turegatan, 18 (D1-2)
Metro östermalmtorg
☎ **08 545 888 88**
Open Mon.-Fri. 10am-6pm, Sat. 11am-4pm.

This Swedish design star has created a relaxed, trendy and practical clothing range for men. The designs are original without being too eccentric, and include well-cut trousers, roomy sweaters, tailored shirts and 1960s-style raincoats.

J Lindeberg

Grev Turegatan, 9 (D1-2)
Metro Östermalmtorg
☎ **08 678 61 65**
Open Mon.-Fri. 10am-6pm, Sat. 11am-4pm.

Imagine John Travolta in a 21st-century version of *Saturday Night Fever* or, simpler still, a Swedish version of Dolce & Gabbana. Anyone who fancies themselves in pink trousers decorated with sequins and spangles, or turquoise suits and flashy striped shirts should head this way. This is one of the top Swedish labels so don't be shy!

Paul & Friends

Grev Turegatan, 7 (D1-2)
Metro Östermalmtorg
☎ **08 54 50 26 50**
Open Mon.-Fri. 10am-6pm, Sat. 11am-4pm.

You'll find a large range of international labels for men in Paul & Friends, including the big Italian names (Gucci, Costume National, Miu Miu and Prada), the German maestro Helmut Lang and the famous English designer Paul Smith. If you fancy something a bit cheaper but just as appealing, however, take a look at the collection of Paul & Friends own label clothes.

Paul & Friends Shoes

Birger Jarlsgatan, on corner with Biblioteksgatan (D2)
Metro Östermalmstorg
☎ 08 54 50 26 25
Open Mon.-Fri. 10am-6pm, Sat. 10am-4pm.

Same name, different product. This branch of Paul & Friends sells international designer shoes for men and women, with Prada and Miu Miu the biggest names on show. It's a chic establishment with a limited selection, high prices and glamorous sales staff.

Björn Borg Clothing

Sergelgatan, 12-14 (C2)
Metro Centralen
☎ 08 217 040
Open Mon.-Fri. 10am-6pm, Sat. 11am-4pm.

Head to Björn Borg's emporium for comfortable underwear, stylish swimwear and chic, colourful, leisure and sportswear, some of it inspired by golfing outfits. Björn's designs for men and women have been equally well received, but they are certainly quite pricey.

IC

Hamngatan, 10 (C2/D2)
Metro Kungsträdgården
☎ 08 242 711
Open Mon.-Fri. 10am-7pm, Sat. 10am-5pm, Sun. noon-4pm.

The men's and women's clothing on sale in this fashion chain are just as good value as those in H&M, but it's not a name that many people have heard of outside

H&M, NK AND AHLÉNS

While the girls are trying on their potential purchases, the boys can browse the rails in H&M and check out the menswear, which has the feel of some of the top international labels. You'll find T-shirts under 100kr, trousers for 300kr, and a good selection of shirts and pullovers. The same goes for NK and Ahléns, each with their own menswear floor boasting a large range of Swedish and international designs.

Sweden. The collection includes the Swedish label Marvin, Clifton and Cam, whose shirts, T-shirts, sweatshirts and accessories hang alongside Levi, Diesel, Wrangler and Lois jeans. It's great for comfortable, everyday wear.

Mr Walker

Norrlandsgatan, 5 (D2)
Metro Kungsträdgården
☎ 08 20 11 20
Open Mon.-Fri. 10am-7pm, Sat. 10am-5pm, Sun. noon-4pm.

Mr Walker is purely a men's clothing store, selling Swedish label jeans and casual wear by famous local designers, including Filippa K, as well as international names such as DKNY and D&G. The Danish label Day and the Icelandic brand Reykjavik are also sold here.

FROM TODDLERS TO TEENS

Swedish children, just like their parents, go to H&M and Filippa K for their clothes. H&M have adorable ranges for babies and children, as well as trendy clothing for teenagers, mostly at reasonable prices. Filippa K sells great outfits for young children in fabulous colours, and prices aren't much more expensive. Toys tend to be made out of either wood or wool, as only 100 per cent natural materials will do.

Sneakersnstuff
Åsögatan, 136 (D3-4)
Metro Medborgarplatsen
☎ 08 743 03 22
Open Mon.-Fri. 11am-6.30pm, Sat. noon-4pm.

Next door to the adult version of the shop, the fun-named 'Sneakersnstuff' sells a wide range of streetwear, including T-shirts, baseball caps and jeans, generally at reasonable prices. You should find everything a young streetwise teenager could possibly need.

Mamma Mia
Humlegårdsgatan, 13/15
Metro Östermalstorg (D2)
☎ 08 667 07 09
Open Mon.-Fri. 10am-6pm, Sat. 10am-3pm.

Mums-to-be come here to buy baby clothes for their new offspring. There's a pretty range from the Swedish company Lycks Mode, including colourful, frilly, and sometimes over-the-top party dresses for 875kr. The woollen baby blankets come in lovely colours and designs (275kr), and the sheepskin linings for prams and pushchairs are worth investing in for chilly winter days (around 600kr).

Kålika
Österlånggatan, 18 (D3)
Metro Gamla Stan
☎ 08 20 52 19
Open Mon.-Fri. 10am-6pm, Sat. 10am-4pm, Sun. noon-4pm.

This small shop has a large selection of wooden toys, including pretty dolls houses and tea sets. You can also take home soft toy animals (blue reindeer 275kr) made from the same fabric as their novelty hats (such as a frog or a penguin, 375kr), or buy a do-it-yourself kit and make your own finger puppets for 95kr. Kålika also sells colourful baby clothes and mobiles. If you have children in tow, you could be here for hours.

BR-Leksaker
Gallerian (at the entrance to the gallery, on the left)
Hamngatan, 37 (C2/D2)
Metro T-Centralen or Kungsträgården
☎ 08 545 15 440
Open Mon.-Fri. 10am-7pm, Sat. 10am-5pm, Sun. noon-4pm.

there are plenty of locally-made wooden toys to choose from, including the Micki construction sets and the painted wooden train sets by Brio. The Pippi Longstocking puzzle is one of the most popular items (299kr). Incomprehensible to adults, it is solved irritatingly quickly by children.

Take your children into this shop at your peril – you won't emerge empty-handed. This two-storey temple to toys caters for children of all ages, even very grown-up ones. Although much of the stock originates from outside Sweden,

Silver House

Götgatan, 38 (D3-4)
Metro Medborgarplatsen
☎ 08 643 09 16
Open Mon.-Fri. noon-6pm, Sat. noon-3pm.

Rödbroka

Hornsgatan, 48 (B3/C3)
Metro Mariatorget
☎ 08 642 16 89
Open Mon.-Fri. 11am-6pm, Sat. 11am-4pm (to 3pm in summer).

This appealing shop is full of ideas for presents to take home, including furry creatures, puppets, Pippi Longstocking puzzles (85-115kr) and wooden toys. One of the nicest items is a market stall, complete with wooden fruit and vegetables.

Dockboden

Svartmangatan, 10 (D3)
Metro Gamla Stan
☎ 08 411 62 34
Open Mon.-Fri. 10am-6pm, Sat. 10am-4pm.

In this tiny workshop/boutique, Catharina Hyttsten sells delightful dolls and teddy bears that she makes and clothes herself. There are some adorable little wooden beds, painted and decorated by Catharina's mother, and tiny porcelain tea sets. If you want to learn how to make the toys yourself, you can take part in one of the courses held in the workshop at the back.

TROLLS AND TOMTARS

Österlånggatan, 45 (D3)
Metro Gamla Stan
☎ 08 10 56 29
Open Mon.-Fri. 11am-6pm, Sat. 11am-3pm (to 4pm in summer).

Maija Tahko and Kicki Floden make fabric figures that have stepped straight out of Swedish fairy tales and legends. Sporting white beards, pointed hats and black attire, they are odd looking creatures. The *tomtar* was said to live around farms, which they would protect as long as they were left undisturbed. If not, terrible things could happen. The hideous trolls stole food and traded their children – ideal for children who love scary things.

For budding starlets everywhere, Silver House has a great selection of costumes, including sparkly sequinned dresses (300kr), Superman outfits, complete with mask and cape, and frilly Spanish flamenco dresses for 600kr.

BEAUTY AND WELL-BEING

The Swedes like to keep healthy, fit and youthful, dedicating much time and energy (and considerable sums of money) in the pursuit of beauty. Jacuzzis, saunas and massages are all part of their daily routine, helping them to relax, feel refreshed and look their best. The new generation of model lookalikes strut the streets of Stockholm – tall, slim, blonde, blue-eyed, with high cheekbones and peachy complexions – in this case the cliché matches the reality.

Opened in 1885 by Dr Carl Curman, these baths are the classiest in Stockholm. Around the main pool, which is really light and airy thanks to the impressive glass roof, there's a cluster of treatment rooms, where you can enjoy an invigorating massage or a relaxing facial.

H&M

Hamngatan, 22 & 14 (C2/D2)
Metro Centralen
☎ 08 79 65 434
Open Mon.-Fri. 10am-7.30pm, Sat. 10am-5pm, Sun. noon-4pm.

This popular brand offers a range of beauty products and in their largest outlet on Hamngatan, there's a wonderful selection of own-brand goodies with which to pamper your face and body and enhance your hair. The prices are pretty painless, which will make you feel even better.

Sturebadet

Sturegallerian, 36 (entrances at Stureplan, 4 and Grev Turegatan, 9/11- D2)
Metro Östermalmstorg
☎ 08 545 015 00
Open Mon.-Fri. 6.30am-10pm, Sat.-Sun. 9am-7pm (25 June-19 Aug. open Mon.-Fri. 6.30am-9pm, Sat.-Sun. 9am-6pm); closed one week in July.

Make-up Store

Drottninggatan, 77 (C2)
Metro Hötorget
☎ 08 411 20 00
Open Mon.-Fri. 10am-6pm, Sat. 11am-5pm.

This cosmetic school has launched its own range of semi-

professional make-up and now boasts five stores in the capital. The demonstrators are all immaculately turned out and will give you a 50-minute lesson on how to create the perfect look for 495kr, including products. They have a vast range of cosmetics, brushes and beauty cases.

Cow

Mäster Samuelsgatan, 9 (C2)
Metro Östermalmstorg
☎ 08 611 15 04
Open Mon.-Fri. 11am-6pm, Sat. 10am-4pm.

Venche Hughes used to be a make-up artist in the world of fashion and cinema and has recently spent much of her time scouring the UK and America for the best professional cosmetics, which she sells in this smart shop with its clinical white interior. Although the range is relatively limited, here you'll find the hottest brands on the international market, such as Urban Decay, Laura Mercier, Vincent Longo and Philosophy.

Lush

Götgatan, 26 (D3-4)
Metro Götgatan
☎ 08 642 00 89
Open Mon.-Fri. 10am-6pm,
Sat. 10am-3pm.

Not surprisingly, for a nation obsessed with health and beauty, Stockholm has its own Lush shop. Just like the UK version, you can smell the colourful array of soaps, shampoos and bath bombs a mile away! All the products are hand-made using natural ingredients and are never tested on animals.

Face Stockholm

Biblioteksgatan, 1 (D2)
Metro Östermalmstorg
☎ 08 611 00 74
Open Mon.-Fri. 10am-6pm,
Sat. 11am-4pm.

Gun Novak and Martina Arfwidson have built up the very successful *Face Stockholm* brand, which now has 8 outlets in the capital,

all designed in what's best described as a 'boudoir' style. Young adults flock to the stores to try out some of the fifty nail varnish and eye shadow colours, which come in attractive black packaging (Drottninggatan, 94, Metro Hötorget, ☎ 08 209 023; Götgatan, 31, Metro Götgatan, ☎ 08 694 91 71).

Stockholm Day Spa

Åhléns City store,
entrance on Mäster
Samuelsgatan, 57
4th floor (C2)
Metro T-Centralen
☎ 08 676 64 50
Open Mon.-Fri. 7am-9pm,
Sat. 10am-7pm.

This spa offers total relaxation and rejuvenation in a new-age environment, with pale wooden floors and muted grey walls. You can indulge in relaxation classes, gentle gym exercises, try out different massages or have a cup of tea before buying some of the beauty products. It's a haven of calm and well-being.

Björn Axen

Åhléns City store, entrance
on Mäster Samuelsgatan, 57,
4th floor (C2)
Metro T-Centralen
☎ 08 545 27 350
(by appt. only).

Next door to the Day Spa, this hairdressing salon, owned by the celebrated stylist Björn Axén, is the only place to get your hair done if you're one of the 'beautiful people'. If you can't afford an impressive and trendy hairstyle, then you can always try the haircare products.

ANTIQUES, DESIGN AND A DASH OF KITSCH

Stockholm boasts some stunning antiques shops, where you may find some interesting treasures, if you're prepared to hunt around. There's a sprinkling of places worth looking at on Köpmangatan, but on the whole, the second-hand stores in Gamla Stan are disappointing. Instead, you should concentrate on the Östermalm district. The design capital has an impressive collection of 20th-century antiques including the best of Scandinavia's creations from the 1950s-1970s.

Rehns

Sibyllegatan, 26 (D1-2)
Metro Stadion
☎ 08 663 34 51
Open Mon.-Fri. 11am-6pm, Sat. 11am-4pm.

Thomas Rehns is an antiques dealer with a shop that looks rather like a theatrical set, complete with revolving mirror-ball lighting. His taste is somewhat eclectic, but his treasures include unusual and often stunning items, sought after by the biggest names in interior design. You'll find furniture and other lovely pieces from Sweden, England, Denmark, Germany and Russia, dating from the 18th, 19th and early 20th centuries.

Lars Thunér

Sibyllegatan, 45 (D1-2)
Metro Stadion
☎ 08 662 52 28
Open Mon.-Fri. noon-6pm, Sat. noon-4pm.

Lars Thunér specialises in antiques dating from the 18th and early 19th centuries, and he stocks some really beautiful Swedish furniture, alongside pieces from other European countries. His Swedish tree-shaped tables and stunning Gustavian chandeliers are not to be missed.

B&L Wahlström

Nybrogatan, 42 (D1-2)
Metro Stadion
☎ 08 662 33 37
Open Mon.-Fri. 11am-5pm, Sat. 11am-4pm.

This is a beautiful shop displaying neo-Classical pieces from Russia and France, objets d'art from the late 18th and early 20th centuries, as well as a large collection of gilded bronze candelabras and mirrors.

Gamla Lampor

Nybrogatan, 3 (D1-2)
Metro Östermalmstorg
☎ 08 611 90 35
Open Mon.-Fri. 11am-5pm, Sat. noon-4pm.

As its name ('Old Lamps') suggests, this is the place to come for lighting in all shapes and sizes. The shop is packed with lamps, including the best in Scandinavian design from the 1950s-1970s. There's also furniture from the Swedish designer Bruno Mathsson, pieces by the Danish stylists Arne Jacobsen, Hans J Wegner and Verner Panton, and the Finnish lamp designer, Alvar Aalto. Ericsson's celebrated 'Ericofon' (telephone) is one of the highlights of the shop. Lovers of great design could easily spend many hours here.

CRYSTAL PERFECTION

Many antiques shops in Stockholm specialise in the magnificent crystal chandeliers from the Gustavian period and the early 19th century. Representing the pinnacle of Swedish decorative art of the time, they come in a variety of styles and sizes. Remember, however, that these items are rare and are therefore very expensive. If you simply want to admire the intricacy of their beauty, you can browse in the following neighbouring shops:

Lars Y Johansson
Kommendörsgatan, 20B
Metro Stadion (D2)
☎ 08 783 03 83.

Lundgrens
Kommendörsgatan, 20A
Metro Stadion (D2)
☎ 08 661 20 00.

Svenska Rum
Nybrogatan, 40 (D1-2)
Metro Stadion
☎ 08 662 17 77.

and focuses principally on Scandinavian design. You'll find an interesting collection of furniture, lights, decorative objects, ceramics and glass on the ground floor, as well as in the 13th-century cellar. Rare limited edition pieces are on display, such as this lacquered wooden clock, designed by the Dane Finn Juhl in 1950 for the United Nations offices in New York.

of fabric. Agnetäs Affär is only open for two hours a day and kitsch reigns supreme, inside and out on the street.

Agnetas Affär

Wollmar Yxkullsgatan, 10
Metro Mariatorget (C3)
☎ 08 699 92 15
Open Mon.-Fri. 4-6pm,
Sat. 1-3pm.

This shop is so tiny and chaotic, that the stock spills onto the pavement outside. The items (mainly from the 1950s-1970s) are unusually arranged by colour, starting with orange. You'll find all sorts of things here, ranging from old-fashioned kitchen equipment to lamps and remnants

Jacksons

Tyska Brinken,
20 (D3)
Metro Gamla Stan
☎ 08 411 85 87
Open Mon.-Fri. noon-6pm,
Sat. 11am-3pm.

Paul and Carina Jackson display the best in design from the Art Nouveau period to the 1990s. They have a huge collection of furniture, lights, ceramics, chairs and other interesting items, all designed by top Scandinavian, Italian and American artists. The shop is not large enough to accommodate all the stock – some is housed in a vast warehouse, which can be visited by appointment. If you're just looking, however, this is not the place for you.

Modernity

Köpmangatan, 3 (D3)
Metro Gamla Stan
☎ 08 20 80 25
Open Mon.-Fri. noon-6pm,
Sat. 11am-3pm.

Andrew Duncanson's collection covers the second half of the 20th century, from the 1940s-1980s,

SWEDISH INTERIOR DESIGN

Fans of interior design will find Stockholm full of choice and innovation. Swedish design is simple and conservative, poetic but practical, combining form with function. Designers employ natural products and use modern industrial techniques alongside traditional craftsmanship. Scandinavian design is at home in the capital, where the shops are full of Swedish, Danish, Norwegian and Finnish products. You'll come across big names as well as less well-known designers, and prices range from the reasonable to the astronomic.

and decorative items. The prices are relatively high but it's worth visiting just for a look.

and useful, and if they fulfil these criteria, then they should also be beautiful. This shop stocks some of the most impressive creations by contemporary Scandinavian designers, some of which appear in the catalogues of major international museums. Some pieces have already become design icons, such as the famous *Block Lamp* by Harri Koskinen (a bulb enclosed in a glass cube), and the slug-shaped bottle opener in brushed aluminium by Calle Hennix. Here you'll find a range of simple, practical items at fairly reasonable prices.

Asplund

Sibyllegatan, 31 (D1-2)
Metro Östermalstorg
☎ 08 662 52 84
Open Mon.-Fri. 10am-6pm, Sat. 10am-4pm.

Designs from Asplund are at the forefront of contemporary Swedish design. These two brothers opened their first studio in 1990, before bringing together their own collection of designs by the cream of Swedish designers, including Thomas Sandell, Jonas Bohlin and Pia Wallen, alongside creations from abroad by Tom Dixon, Antonio Citterio and Marc Newson. The gallery is home to the celebrated woollen rugs (a house speciality) in fabulous colours and shapes, together with furniture

Design House

Karlavägen, 73 (D1-2)
Metro Stadion
☎ 08 545 012 25
Open Mon.-Fri. 10am-6pm, Sat. 10am-4pm.

The mission statement of the Design House is that one should only make items that are both necessary

Linnehuset

Narvavägen, 34 (D2)
Metro Karlaplan
☎ 08 661 09 55
Open Mon.-Fri. 10am-6pm, Sat. 11am-4pm
(closed for lunch 2-3pm).

Linnehuset only sells top quality linen that is excellent value for money. Available by the metre in different colours, or sold as tablecloths, napkins, tea towels, clothes, pyjamas, bed linen, towels and massage gloves. Among the highlights are the checked napkins in pure Swedish linen, made by Klässbols, which are perfect for the Christmas table and make lovely presents to take home.

Solgården
Karlavägen, 58 (D1-2)
Metro Stadion
☎ **08 663 93 60**
Open Mon.-Fri. 10am-6pm,
Sat. 10am-4pm.

Marianne von Kantzow Ridderstad offers her own interpretation of Gustavian country style in this charming shop, with its tasteful cool, white interior and feeling for the past. Although Solgården displays some antique pieces, it mainly specialises in its own collection of painted wooden reproduction furniture with trompe l'oeil motifs and white cotton drapes. It also sells attractive white chinaware, hand-blown glass, lamps, linen and a small collection of giftware and accessories for babies.

Design Torget
Kulturhuset
Sergels Torg (C2)
Metro T-Centralen
☎ **08 508 315 20**
Open Mon. 11am-7pm,
Tues.-Fri. 10am-7pm, Sat.
10am-5pm, Sun. 11am-5pm.

Interior designer and architect, Jerry Hellström and consultant John Hamberg, came together with a specific concept in mind – to establish a place in which they could showcase the work of young artisans and designers. Design Torget rents out space to different designers every few months, guaranteeing regular exposure of new work. You'll find kitchen and bathroom accessories, storage equipment

and plates and dishes on display. Every two years new designers are commissioned to create ideas based on a particular theme. The results are exhibited and the best work goes into production There's also a store at Götgatan, 31 (D3-4, Metro Slussen, ☎ 08 462 35 20).

Marimekko
Årstaängsvägen, 31 G (B4)
Metro Kungsträdgården
☎ **08 794 07 30**
Open Mon.-Fri. 10am-6pm,
Sat. 10am-4pm.

This famous Finnish label, immensely popular in the 1960s, celebrated 50 years of business in 2001. Here, in its first store outside Finland, you'll find colourful fabrics by Maija Isola and new collections by her daughter Kristina, who has taken over the creative baton. The collection includes bed linen, bath towels, shower curtains, beachwear and clothing. Fun designs with flowers, stripes and polka dots make this a cheerful if quite pricey range.

Zero Pukeberg

Nybrogatan, 16 (D1-2)
Metro Östermalmstorg
☎ 08 545 850 02
Open Mon.-Fri. 10am-6pm,
Sat. 10am-4pm.

Furniture, glass and lighting are
the three key lines in Zero. Behind
the narrow shop frontage lies a
huge, deep gallery supported by
exposed concrete pillars. Here
the best Swedish designers are
commissioned to create stunning,
limited edition or one-off pieces,
such as vases and glasses
(transparent and coloured), that
are hand-blown and crafted in
pure Swedish tradition. The glass
lights by Thomas Sandell are
particularly beautiful.

Silent Statement

Luntmakargatan, 50 (C1-2)
Metro Rådmansgatan
☎ 08 673 60 80
Open Mon.-Fri. noon-8pm,
Sat. noon-6pm.

Mats Ohlson
welcomes you into
his shop as if it
were his own
home, offering
you the chance
to enjoy a coffee
or a glass of
organic fruit
juice and relax
for a few minutes.
His eclectic
collection is in
constant flux and well

worth a browse. You'll find plates,
dishes, candleholders, kitchen
and bathroom accessories, many
of which are limited editions, and
all gift-wrapped in boxes filled
with confetti. This is the perfect
spot to buy a very original gift
without breaking the bank.

Plan ett

Tegnérgatan, 13 (C1-2)
Metro Rådmansgatan
☎ 08 555 297 07
Open Mon.-Fri. 10am-6pm,
Sat. 10am-4pm.

Plan ett is both a shop and a
gallery focusing on interior
design. Here you'll find the work
of young designers yet to make
their name, mostly of Swedish
origin but also from England,
Holland, Denmark and Finland.
There's a common theme to the
decorative items, furniture, rugs
and mirrors on display – all
the objects are functional.
The prices are quite
reasonable too.

Bruka design

Östermalms Saluhall
Humlegårdsgatan, 1 (D2)
Metro Östermalstorg
☎ 08 660 14 80
Open Mon.-Fri. 10am-6pm,
Sat. 10am-4pm.

This shop, spread over two floors,
sells charming household items,
including kitchen utensils and
attractive wicker baskets. It also
stocks cane furniture and kitchen
linen and is a great place to come
and browse.

Nordiska Kristall

Kungsgatan, 9 (C2)
Metro Östermalmstorg
☎ 08 10 43 72.

Kristall Butiken

Österlånggatan, 13 (D3)
Metro Gamla Stan
☎ 08 24 26 86.

Two shops, two different names,
but all one family. The Kjellanders
first opened a store in 1922, and
they still boast the largest
and best collection of
traditional Swedish
glass and crystal,
including names
like Kosta Boda,
Orrefors and
Måleräs. Danish
designs by Georg
Jensen and
Royal

Copenhagen are also represented, together with the work of Venetian artist, Venini. The collections include fine glassware, some hand painted, and attractive decorated plates. In the basement of the first shop, Nordiska Kristall, you'll find a gallery housing temporary exhibitions of unique pieces.

Georg Jensen

Birger Jarlsgatan, 13 (C1-2)
Metro Östermalmstorg
☎ 08 545 040 80
Open Mon.-Fri. 10am-6pm,
Sat. 10am-4pm.

Georg Jensen is a big name both in his native Denmark and abroad. His stylish silverware is renowned for its pure and sophisticated lines. His collection includes stunning silver and gold jewellery,

watches, clocks and decorative items. The prices match the quality, so you may just want to look on in admiration.

David Design

Nybrogatan, 7 (D1-2)
Metro Östermalmstorg
☎ 08 611 91 55
Open Mon.-Fri. 10am-
6pm, Sat. 10am-4pm.

This young company from Malmö opened its first studio in Stockholm in 2000. Best described as a 'concept store', it has white walls, black wooden floor and huge range of household items.

The first thing you see as you walk in the door is the bar, where you can enjoy a cappuccino. Further on is a bookshop with a large selection of lounge music CDs and books on cookery, design and architecture. The main part of the shop sells crockery, cutlery, kitchen items and even clothes to wear about the house. Pia Wallen's exceptional felt bags are on sale, alongside beauty products and rugs. This place is a true showcase for the new spirit in Swedish design.

Norrvagel

Birger Jarlsgatan, 27 (C1-2)
Metro Östermalmstorg
☎ 08 545 220 59
Open Mon.-Fri. 10am-6pm,
Sat. 10am-4pm.

Norrvagel extends over three floors and is a favourite haunt of locals in search of trendy ideas for the home. It sells a vast array of useful items including furniture and accessories, designed in a simple, country style with a contemporary touch, inspired by nature itself. The natural and painted wooden furniture, mirrors and shelving are very attractive, and the natural fabrics in matching colours are equally wonderful. There are even some very cosy looking real sheepskin cushions.

DEPARTMENT STORES AND SHOPPING MALLS

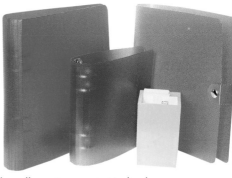

Shopaholics should head straight for the two large, well-known department stores – NK and Åhléns – before going on to visit some of the other popular shopping malls. Luckily these all operate convenient trading hours and are open on a Sunday afternoon, so you can shop till you drop.

DEPARTMENT STORES

NK (Nordiska Kompaniet)

Hamngatan, 18-20 (C2/D2)
Metro Kundsträdgården
☎ 08 76 29 000
Open Mon.-Fri. 10am-7pm (basement food hall to 8pm), Sat. 10am-5pm (basement to 6pm), Sun. noon-5pm (to 4pm in June & July).

The huge, rotating clock at the top of the NK store has, without a doubt, become one of the symbols of the city. Nordiska Kompaniet is a shopping mecca in the capital and sells practically everything, from beauty products and fashion to hi-fi systems and food, not forgetting the travel agency, flower

shop and café. No trip to the capital would be complete without a visit to this formidable store.

Åhléns City

Klarabergsgatan, 50 (C2)
Metro T-Centralen
Open Mon.-Fri. 10am-7pm, Sat. 10am-6pm, Sun. noon-4pm.

This store is just as attractive as NK, but is housed in a more contemporary building. Among its many attractions are all the major clothing labels sold in individual concessions. You'll also find household items and furniture, as well as a wonderful food hall in the basement, which is definitely worth a visit.

PUB

Drottninggatan, 72-76 (C2)
Metro Hötorget
Open Mon.-Fri. 10am-7pm, Sat. 10am-5pm, Sun. noon-5pm.

Even more popular than NK and Åhléns, PUB is a large store not far from Hötorget, operating in two buildings located on opposite sides of Drottninggatan. Almost an institution in Stockholm (Greta Garbo once modelled hats for the store's spring catalogue), it sells everything you could possibly want for yourself or your home, including a large range of CDs for those who want to check out the latest movements in the Swedish music charts. There's also an internet café on the top floor where you can relax, have a drink and email your friends back home.

SHOPPING MALLS

Sturegallerian

Entrances Strureplan, 4 and Grev Turegatan, 9/11 (D2) Open Mon.-Fri. 10am-7pm, Sat. 10am-5pm, Sun. 10am-5pm.

Located right in the centre of the shopping district, Sturegallerian is home to several big fashion labels and interior design companies including Björn Borg, J Lindeberg and Ordning&Reda. You can also enjoy a massage or moment of relaxation at Sturebadet (see p. 55). On Friday evenings, the young and trendy gather at Stures Restaurang for a drink (open Mon.-Fri. 10am-11pm, Sat. 10am-8pm, Sun. noon-8pm) or dine at Sturehof and O-Baren. At lunchtime, the Gateau café on the first floor of Sturegallerian is full of young mums with pushchairs.

PK Huset

Entrance through the basement of NK and on the corner of Norrlandsgatan and Smålandsgatan (D2) Open Mon.-Fri. 10am-7pm, Sat. 10am-5pm, Sun. noon-4pm.

This is a popular mall, largely due to its location next to the NK shop, through which you can also gain access. The mall is home to a number of mid-range fashion boutiques.

Gallerian

Hamngatan, 37 (C2/D2) Metro T-Centralen or Kungsträgården Open Mon.-Fri. 10am-7pm, Sat. 10am-6pm, Sun. 11am-4pm.

Gallerian houses some sixty stores, restaurants and cafés, with a variety of generally good value shops selling clothes, shoes, music, home electronics, etc. Its main attraction, however, is the huge toyshop, BR-Leksaker (at the entrance to the mall, on the left),

CITY SHOPPING

Sveavagen, 9 (C1-2) Open Mon.-Fri. 10am-7pm, Sat. 10am-5pm.

At the foot of the City's rectangular towers, the ground floor is home to a number of chic fashion stores and bars, where employees come at the end of the day to relax. Both summer and winter, even when their breath freezes in the air, you'll find 'suits' enjoying a quick coffee and a smoke out on the pavement, escaping the strict no-smoking regulation in their offices.

which stocks an impressive collection of toys in all shapes and sizes and as for all age groups, as well as a whole section devoted to Lego.

FOOD AND MARKETS

You can buy a delicious range of food in the markets (indoor and outdoor) in Stockholm, as well as in the food halls and supermarkets located in the large department stores, so it's worth taking a look. Once you've sampled some of the local specialities, you'll have a better idea of the kind of products that will make unusual and delicious gifts to take back home.

Östermalms Saluhall

Östermalmstorg, on the corner of Humlegårdsgatan and Nybrogatan (D2)
Open Mon.-Thurs. 9.30am-6pm, Fri. 9.30am-6.30pm, Sat. 9.30am-2pm.

Prepare yourself for a journey of sensory delight in this covered market hall, which boasts a veritable feast of goodies. Housed in a 19th-century red brick building, around 30 stalls sell a range of traditional Swedish gastronomic delights, including smoked reindeer meat, cheese, charcuterie and smoked or marinated salmon, all of which can be vacuum-packed to take home. The fruit and flower stalls are particularly impressive, and if you're wandering around at lunchtime, you'll find it almost

impossible to resist the tempting snacks on offer. Watch out for the prices, though!

Ingelska Kalkon

Humlegårdsgatan, 13 (D2)
☎ 08 660 33 66
Open Mon.-Fri. 10am-6pm, Sat. 10am-2pm.

Not far from Östermalms Saluhall is Ingelska Kalkon, a wonderful shop bursting with gastronomic temptations. Everything on sale is produced locally and made from turkey meat, including turkey pâtés, sausages, roasts, meatballs and sliced cooked fillets.

Highlights include the pastrami, smoked turkey thighs and the liver pâté, and you can buy mustards and other condiments to complement them. If you're peckish you can stay here and enjoy a set meal for 35-70kr.

Rosendals

Rosendalsterassen, 12 (E2)
☎ 08 545 812 70
Open 1 Oct.-30 Apr. Tue.-Sun. 10am-4pm; 1 May-30 Sept. every day 10am-6pm.

The delightful Rosendals garden (see p. 64) has its own shop and café, situated in a greenhouse and surrounded by a lovely kitchen garden and fruit orchard. Here you'll find a range of organic fruit, vegetables, fruit juices, jams, chutneys and honey. Everything is 100 per cent natural, wholesome and delicious.

CHRISTMAS MARKETS

Once December arrives, Stockholm's festive Christmas markets start to appear. The largest and most traditional is Skansen, located in the open-air village museum on the three Sundays leading up to Christmas (11am-6pm). The market in the Old Town, on Stortorget (D3, in front of the Nobel Museum, open every day 1-23 December, 11am-6pm), has charming gifts for Christmas and St Lucia's Day (13 December), while Rosendal's Christmas market (E2, open every day Nov. 24-Dec. 19), sells decorations, wreaths and crafts.

There has traditionally been a market on this site since 1640. Just outside the hall lies Hörtorget, Scandinavia's largest market square, with its lively daily market selling fruit, vegetables and flowers. On Sundays temporary vendors take over the square trading in books, household gadgets and oddments.

NK and Åhléns

In the basements of both these department stores (see p. 104), you'll find huge, wonderful foodhalls selling fresh fish and meat, along with local specialities such as traditional sauces, tubes of prawn pâté and Swedish caviar. There's no point looking for beer or vodka, though, since alcohol can only be bought at the official Bolaget stores (see p. 26).

Göta Fisk

Götgatan, 96 (D3-4)
☎ 08 640 67 89
Open Mon.-Fri. 10am-6pm,
Sat. 9.30am-2pm.

Although you may not be able to take fresh herring home with you in your suitcase, this shop is still worth a visit, if only just to admire the amazing selection of fresh fish on offer. It's the perfect place to buy food for a picnic, as there's a delicatessen counter selling a wide selection of prepared dishes

and special sauces, cooked to secret Swedish recipes with unusual names.

Hötorgshallen

Hötorget (C2)
Open Mon.-Wed. 10am-6pm,
Thurs.-Fri. 10am-7pm, Sat.
10am-4pm.

This market hall, built in the 1950s and renovated in the 1990s, has an exciting selection of Swedish and exotic specialities.

Söderhallarna

Medborgarplatsen (D3)
Open Mon.-Wed. 10am-6pm,
Thurs.-Fri. 10am-7pm, Sat.
10am-4pm.

Located on Söder Square, this market is a modern version of Östermalms Saluhall, with stalls selling fresh produce and counters serving pasta salad. It's not as attractive as Östermalm, but is still a pleasant place to wander around.

ARTS AND CRAFTS

Traditional handicrafts continue to be popular in Sweden, but the work of contemporary artisans is considered equally important, particularly by the younger generations. Like its design counterpart, the local arts and crafts embody the Swedish spirit, taking inspiration from the natural world. Glass, ceramics, wood and fabrics are the principal media used to create simple, colourful and very beautiful pieces.

turns to sell the pieces in-between working in their studios. Look out for Eva Skarbäck's attractive, colourful fruit bowls, which would make a great gift to take back home.

Blås&Knåda

Horsngatan, 26 (B3/C3)
Metro Slussen
☎ 08 642 77 67
Open Mon.-Fri. 11am-6pm,
Sat. 11am-4pm, Sun.
noon-4pm.

This enormous gallery exhibits the work of around fifty ceramic artists and glassblowers, offering a collection of limited edition series and one-off pieces at a range of prices. There are simple, hand-painted mugs and bowls, striking hand-blown glass vases and even ceramic furniture.

Kaolin

Hornsgatan, 50 (B3/C3)
Metro Mariatorget
☎ 08 644 46 00
Open Tue.-Fri. 11am-6pm,
Sat. 11am-4pm.

The Kaolin gallery specialises in ceramics, displaying the work of around twenty artists, grouped together in a co-operative (this is quite usual, even if there is a wide variety in styles). The artists take

Handarbetets Vänner Licium

Djurgårdsslätten, 82-84 (E3)
Bus no. 47, opposite the
main entrance to Skansen
☎ 08 667 10 26
Open Tue.-Sat. noon-4pm.

Tradition and renewal are the key themes of 'The Association for Friends of Textile Art', which has been in existence since 1874; the gallery itself arranges exhibitions (on occasions, somewhat experimental) of contemporary textile design. Special commissions are completed in the workshop, and are often unique and quite unusual, such as giant tapestries or rugs. These are usually made for institutions and private clients, including museums, concert venues and conference halls. There's a small shop situated inside the gallery selling beautiful skeins of wool, dyed with natural pigments by members of the association.

and is available by the metre. In the basement you'll find temporary exhibitions showcasing the work of talented, up-and-coming apprentice designers.

Textilarna

Österlånggatan, 25 (D3)
Metro Gamla Stan
☎ 08 411 03 53
Open Mon.-Fri. 11am-6pm,
Sat. 11am-3pm.

This small yet impressive shop, situated on one of the main streets of the Old Town, sells the imaginative and humorous creations of five textile artists. The fabrics are all hand-printed and the designs are original and sold in limited edition series. There are T-shirts, small trays and cushions, as well as some adorable baby clothes, designed with either motifs such as pirates or smiley faces (230kr).

Swedish Tourist Office shop

Hamngatan, 27 (C2/D2)
Metro Kundsträdgården
Open Mon.-Fri.
8am-7pm, Sat.-Sun.
9am-5pm.

This is the perfect place for a spot of last minute shopping. The Swedish Tourist Office shop is full of souvenirs, small gifts and traditional handicrafts. The brightly coloured furry reindeers make an ideal gift for young children and the Dalecarlia painted wooden horses are really attractive. These are available in bright red or royal blue, with floral harnesses.

Agata

Nytorgsgatan, 36 (D3-4)
Metro Medbodgarplatsen
☎ 08 643 09 80
Open Mon.-Fri. 11am-6pm,
Sat. 11am-3pm.

This small shop sells limited editions of handmade pieces created by young designers. Take a look at Kinnasand's super furnishing fabric made from printed cotton. It comes in a wonderful range of colours, decorated with 1970s-style motifs,

MUSEUM SHOPS

Stockholm's museum shops sell a wonderful range of Swedish handicrafts. The Skansen shop (Djurgårdsslätten, E3, bus no. 47. Open every day 11am-4pm, to 7pm in June, July and Aug.), is located next to the main entrance to the park and has a huge range of small, traditional objects at great prices. The National Art Museum shop (Blasieholmshamnen, D2, metro Kungsträdgården. Open Tues. 11am-8pm, Wed.-Sun. 11am-5pm), situated just before the Skeppsholmsbron bridge, offers a great selection of items in conjunction with its temporary exhibitions, such as hand-printed textiles, glassware, trays, table decorations and design classics such as the glass salad bowl designed for Stelton by Arne Jacobsen. Keep an eye on the prices.

Bargains and surprises in store

Stockholm is full of unusual shops and bargains galore, so it's worth bringing an empty suitcase with you if you plan to go on a spending spree. The best shops for a good rummage can be found to the south of the city, where the streets of Södermalm are dotted with boutiques selling second-hand goods.

Kronan Cynel Svenska AB

Birger Jarlsgatan, 37 (C1-2)
Metro
Östermalmstorg
☎ 08 694 72 82
Open Mon.-Fri. 11am-6.30pm, Sat. noon-4pm.

Not far from Stureplan, this small shop sells just one item – a former army-issue bicycle, but in a wide range of colours and styles and sporting a new and contemporary look.

The solid, comfortable 'city bike' is sold for between 2,795kr (for the 2-gear model) and 3,495kr (with 3 gears). Every self-respecting, stylish cyclist in the capital should have one.

Stockholms Dansservice

Hornsgatan, 71 (B3/C3)
Metro Zinkensdamn
☎ 08 669 49 10
Open Mon.-Fri. 10am-6pm, Sat. 10am-3pm (closes at 1pm on Sat. in July).

Dance enthusiasts, whether amateur or professional, will find everything they could possibly want here, whether they're into ballet, tango, jazz, flamenco, or ballroom dancing. It's a riot of colour inside, and sells everything from traditional ballet tutus and shocking pink ostrich feather boas, to professional stage make-up and tap shoes.

Magnus von Brömssen

Stora Nygatans Antiques
Stora Nygatan, 39 (C3/D3)
Metro Gamla Stan
☎ 08 22 65 03
Open Mon.-Fri. 10am-5pm, Sat. noon-4pm.

This extraordinary shop is a veritable jungle, brimming with items from the past, among them numerous piles of books and a large quantity of Russian army uniforms. Between 1860 and 1940, Sweden was the main manufacturer of matches, exporting them to five continents.

There were no fewer than 25,000 different makes at the time and Magnus von Brömssen has a fair number of examples on show. You could easily spend many hours here, so make sure you allow yourself enough time for a proper rummage.

Rey Urban

Sibyllegatan, 49 (D1-2)
Metro Stadion
☎ 08 662 55 66
Open Mon.-Fri. 10am-5pm, Sat. 11am-4pm.

Since 1995, this studio-cum-boutique has been making and selling wonderful jewellery and contemporary pieces in silver and gold. The designs are simple and pure in style, exceptionally elegant and are created using traditional techniques. It's a delightful place just to come for a look around, although you may find it difficult to resist some of the lovely and original creations they have to offer.

Fancy House, Dressed for Success

Götgatan, 14 (D3-4)
Metro Slussen
☎ 08 640 10 69
Open Mon.-Fri. 10am-7pm, Sat. 11am-4pm.

If you enjoy dressing up and fancy yourself as one of Madonna's backing singers, a Las Vegas-style entertainer, an exotic dancer or a member of the Chippendales, then look no further. This shop stocks everything you could possibly need to transform yourself, with a wide range of extravagant outfits, including fur trousers, studded leather jackets and glitzy bikinis. It's more kitsch than haute couture, but worth having a look all the same.

STOCKHOLM QUALITY OUTLET

On the outskirts of the city, not far from Arlanda airport and about forty minutes from the centre, is a vast factory outlet centre, where you can choose from over sixty different boutiques featuring a wide range of clothes, shoes and accessories from both Swedish and international labels, and all at unbeatable prices. Aquascutum, Björn Borg, Filippa K, Dockers, Design House, Diesel, Ording&Reda, Samsonite, Tommy Hilfiger – they're all here. It's a real mecca for shopaholics, and you're sure to find some real bargains with prices 30-60% lower than normal. Take the Barkaby train to Jakobsberg and then bus no. 567 to Barkaby Handelsplats, next to Ikea. The shopping centre (☎ 08 564 720 31) is open Mon.-Fri. 11am-8pm, Sat. 10am-5pm, Sun. 11am-5pm.

Robbyge

Grev Turegatan, 20 (D1-2)
Metro Östermalmstorg
☎ 08 667 79 69
Open Mon.-Fri. 10am-6pm,
Sat. 10am-4pm.

This shop is entirely run along
the principles laid down by Rudolf
Steiner, the 20th-century German
educationalist, whose ideas and
philosophy have a huge following
in Sweden. He advocated that
everything we consume should be
100 per cent natural, so all the
toys at Robbyge are made of wood
and the children's clothes are
made from pure cotton or linen.
Similarly, the cosmetics are all

Ruby Vintage Clothing

Wollmar Yxkullsgatan, 9 (C3)
Metro Mariatorget
☎ 08 640 72 92
Open Mon.-Fri. noon-6pm,
Sat. noon-4pm.

Walking into this store is like
stepping back into an American
college in the 1970s. This is the
shop owner's favourite era, so
take your time and have a good
look through his collection of
1970s music and browse the
tightly-packed racks filled with
two-toned American university
bomber jackets, colourful T-shirts
and jeans.

the leather jackets, shoes, jeans
and T-shirts on sale. The prices
are pretty well unbeatable.

completely natural and the toy kits
are made of naturally dyed felt.
Steiner's principles are applied to
the shop just as
they are in his
schools.

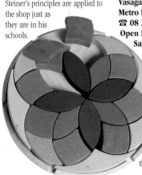

Uff

Vasagatan, 26 (C2)
Metro Hötorget
☎ 08 24 20 06
Open Mon.-Fri. 10am-6pm,
Sat. 10am-4pm.

This huge shop is
brimming with
second-hand clothes
for both men and
women. If you have
the time and
patience to look
through the huge
stock, you may well
come across the find of
the century, hidden among

Vintage Guitars

Götgatan, 28 (D3-4)
Metro Slussen
☎ 08 643 10 83
Open Mon.-Fri. 11am-6pm,
Sat. 11am-4pm.

No prizes for guessing the passion
shared by the owners of this shop,
Rikard Magnevill and Claes
Parmland. It's worth having a
careful look at the different guitar
models, which are generally of
the highest quality and sometimes
even include a few rare examples.
There are a large number of
American electric guitars on sale,
as well as a few Swedish ones

Located in Djurgården, between the Vasa museum and the Liljevalchs gallery, this outlet is housed on the first floor of a large warehouse with a bright red roof, and is only open in summer. It sells a vast range of jeans and seasonal sportswear for men and women, mostly from across the Atlantic (including such makes as California Girl, Santa Cruz and Weather Report), or from the Swedish Svea label.

OUTDOOR GEAR

The Swedes love the great outdoors and most of them have all the necessary equipment to enjoy it to the full. If you want to stock up on some heavy duty gear, check out these two great shops that sell the well-known Swedish label, Fjäll Räven. Take your pick from rucksacks, travelling accessories, sleeping bags (from 699kr), tents, fishing gear, canoeing and rafting equipment, multi-purpose Leatherman knives, camping cutlery or vacuum-packed food.

dating from 1940-1980, with prices ranging from 1,500kr to 100,000kr (or even more for the rare or unique models).

Second Hand

Hornsgatan, 29C (B3/C3)
Metro Mariatorget
Open Mon.-Fri. 11am-6pm,
Sat. 11am-2pm.

Interestingly, this second-hand shop focuses solely on children – the shelves are stuffed full of clothes, shoes and toys for little ones aged 0-10, some even sporting famous labels. All the stock is in excellent condition and the prices are just as appealing. Now is the time to dress the fashionistas of the future in vintage wear.

Kungliga Djurgårdens Outlet

Wasa Hallen
(next to the Vasamuseet, D2)
Bus no. 47
Open June-mid Aug. every day 11am-7pm.

Natuur Kompaniet
Kungsgatan, 4 A (C2)
Metro Hötorget
☎ **08 723 15 81**
Open Mon.-Fri. 10am-6pm, Sat. 10am-3pm.

FriluftsBolaget
Sveavägen 62 (C1-2)
Metro SL-hittegods
☎ **08 24 30 02**
Open Mon.-Fri. 10am-6pm, Sat. 10am-3pm.

Nightlife practicalities

Stockholm's nightlife is focused in two key areas – the city centre, around Stureplan and its famous white mushroom, where cool and chic locals meet up for a night out, and Södermalm, between Hornsgatan and Mosebacke Torg, where things are more relaxed and have an arty feel. You won't have any difficulty finding somewhere with the right atmosphere, whatever the time of year, and you'll soon discover that the Swedes are real party animals.

WHERE IT ALL HAPPENS

An evening out in Stockholm nearly always seems to start at the popular *Svampen*, the Stureplan 'mushroom' building (see p. 54), which is so distinctive (some might say ugly) that you can't possibly miss it. This is the main meeting place for the capital's young people and you'll see them standing here, shuffling around to keep warm as they wait for their chums to turn up. Dinner takes place relatively early (from 5pm onwards and rarely later than 8pm if you are eating in a restaurant), but the nightly tour of the bars doesn't start until about 11pm, and the nightclubs don't get going until even later. There are plenty of cultural events happening all over the capital, from

large-scale operatic and theatrical performances, to classical music concerts held in local churches, rock gigs in large venues, cabaret and intimate jazz nights. Going to the cinema should not be a problem for non-Swedish speakers, since most films are shown in the original language with Swedish subtitles, and there are plenty of American, British or 'arthouse' movies to choose

from. The Swedish film industry is less prolific than it once was, however, and its output does tend to be rather intellectual. The Södermalm district, meanwhile, is rather cooler and more trendy, offering a modern take on the old classics, such as rock 'n' roll versions of major works by international playwrights and composers, and new contemporary interpretations by independent theatre groups. The nightlife in general is pretty intense, arty and bohemian, but in a very Swedish way.

FINDING OUT WHAT'S ON

The Swedish Tourist Office is a good place to start if you want to know where to go, what to see and how to get tickets. They also have a very efficient booking office. Try to get your hands on a copy of the incredibly useful monthly publication *What's On*, which details all the main events, categorised by genre (jazz, rock, classical music, opera etc.) and date. If you aren't anywhere near the Swedish Tourist Office (located in Hamngatan), however, you can buy tickets – along with newspapers, cigarettes and sweets – in some of the Pressbyro kiosks, recognisable by their ATG sign (a blue logo featuring a horse). Tickets are also available at the main train station, on Drottninggatan, and in various other venues across the city. You can check programmes on the internet at www.stockholmtown.com (the website of the Stockholm Information Service), or head for the Box Office kiosk on Norrmalmstorg square, near the theatre (☎ 08 10 88 10, ☏ 08 545 169 10, website: www.boxoffice.se).

THE DRESS CODE

No offence intended, but if you're over 25 in Sweden, you are generally considered to be quite old. Only the very young strut their stuff on the dance floors, although some of the more trendy types from the world of art, media and journalism (along with those who refuse to grow old) do sometimes boogie on down and join in the fun. In general, the Swedes like to live life to the full until the ripe old age of 25, and then settle down, get married and have children. After this, they rarely go out as a couple, since one or other of them generally does the babysitting, meaning that groups of male or female partygoers are quite common. Fortunately, this ageism does not apply to theatres, concerts or restaurants, where you can happily enjoy yourself without worrying too much about your age.

Young people tend to live with their parents, which means they can afford to spend money on their clothes and wear big brand labels. Many of them look as if they have just stepped off the pages of a magazine or a CD cover, although their 'look' can often appear rather uniform. You don't need to worry too much about what you wear, although you will probably need a tie if you plan to dine in a top restaurant such as the Operakällaren, and in some venues jeans and trainers can be sniffed at. Most important of all though, is a warm coat, as it can get quite chilly at night, even in summer. In many bars, discos and pubs, you're required to leave your coat in the cloakroom (at a cost of around 10kr).

SAFETY

You should feel pretty safe wandering around the streets of Stockholm at night. The crime rate in the capital is extremely low and you shouldn't have to worry about your purse, wallet or jewellery when you're out and about. In the evening, you can enjoy a walk along the water's edge (along Södermalm Mälarstrand, for example), without being concerned about your personal safety. Walking back to your hotel at night is also generally a safe option, and in the summer, it's almost daylight by 3am.

SHOWS

Stockholm Jazz Festival

There's plenty going on in Stockholm during the summer, including several open-air festivals. The largest of these is the week-long jazz festival, held annually in mid-July on the island of Skeppsholmen. It has an international reputation and stars from the world of jazz, blues, soul and latin music regularly take part. Less famous names perform on a smaller stage nearby. The restaurant in the Moderna Museet (Museum of Modern Art), Kantin Moneo, hosts 'Jam Session Nights', during which you can enjoy the music, as well as the spectacular view over Djurgården.

In addition, the very short nights, which last only a few hours, make the atmosphere quite special. You can buy your tickets in advance on the internet: www.stockholmjazz.com

What's in What's On

The free listings magazine *What's On* is a bilingual Swedish/English monthly published by the Stockholm Information Service. With all kinds of useful information, it features a comprehensive monthly calendar of events, with details of classical music concerts in churches, rock and jazz concerts, shows, operatic performances, and dinner and jazz evenings on Lake Mälaren and in the archipelago. You can get hold of a copy from the Swedish Tourist Office (Hamngatan, 27, entrance on the corner with Kungsträdgården) or from your hotel reception.

Cirkus

Djurgårdsslätten (E3)
Info: ☎ 08 660 10 20.

This former circus dates back to the early 20th century and has become a venue for a variety of popular events, including contemporary music hall, Chippendale-style male striptease acts and rock and pop concerts. Its exterior has been well preserved and is pretty impressive.

Dansens Hus

Barnhusgatan, 12/14 (C2)
☎ 08 665 80 18.

Built in the 1960s, this temple to modern dance is home to contemporary dance companies. It has an impressive stage set

and an interesting programme, including the work of Swedish choreographers.

Dramaten (Royal Dramatic Theatre)

Nybroplan (D2)
☎ **08 667 06 80.**

This building, formerly nick-named the 'White Temple', is an Art Nouveau masterpiece, its lovely gilding and ceilings painted by Carl Larsson inspired by Viennese style of the time. Its programme focuses on classical Swedish drama, including the works of the influential and provocative Swedish playwright, August Strindberg. The actors who have graced its stage include the legendary Greta Garbo.

Mosebacke Etablissement

Mosebacke Torg, 3 (D3)
☎ **08 556 098 90.**

Since the 19th century, the Mosebacke Etablissement has been the cultural heart of Söder. The greatest Swedish artists made their debut here and their portraits now hang on the walls of the foyer. This multicultural centre is a favourite meeting place for Stockholm's culture vultures, with a great atmosphere and lively programme of drama, jazz and classical concerts, which are held in two small auditoria next to the theatre. The shows alternate with themed evenings – so on Thursdays it's salsa night.

Kulturhuset

Sergels Torg (C2)
☎ **08 508 315 08.**

This vast auditorium is dedicated to promoting contemporary culture and hosts a range of different events, including music and drama, most of which are modern (see p. 56).

Operan

Karl XII Torget (D2)
☎ **08 791 43 00.**

This very majestic 19th-century building, home to Swedish opera, was built to replace the former 18th-century Baroque edifice which was destroyed by fire. Along with the theatre in

Nybroplan, it's the most chic arts venue in the city, offering locals the chance to enjoy classical ballet and opera staged within its impressive walls (see p. 56).

Biografen Sture

Birger Jarlsgatan, 28-30 (C1-2/D2)
☎ 08 678 85 48.

Cinemas are incredibly popular in Sweden, and this one is no exception. The arty decor in the foyer makes it as interesting a venue as the cinema itself, and you can enjoy a leisurely drink here before the film. The programme is very focused and

is organised in specific, themed cycles. Generally it features films from outside Sweden, which are screened in their original language with Swedish subtitles.

The Green Room

Götgatan, 55 (D3-4)
☎ 08 556 920 00
Closed July.

This 1960s-style cinema is located in the trendy Södermalm district and includes a rock concert venue and nightclub. It has a great atmosphere and you can enjoy a cocktail or a snack here before the film.

Globen

Globen Torget, 2 (off map)
☎ 08 725 10 00.

Located to the extreme south of the city, Globen's enormous metal dome is clearly visible in the distance, even from the hills of Söder. This vast concert arena is the venue for some of the greatest international names in rock, such as Bruce Springsteen and U2, as well as hosting contemporary musical concerts, shows and dance spectaculars.

BARS

Bar à Vin

Smålandsgatan, 11 (D2)
☎ 08 678 10 30
Open Mon.-Sat. 5-11pm.

No prizes for guessing what's served in the Riche restaurant's new annexe, with its minimalist interior subtly decorated with stone and wood. The surprise, however, lies in its very extensive and impressive wine list. The wines come from all over the world and you can to order a

Handy to know

Until recently, there was a strict regulation in Sweden that prohibited the sale of alcohol without food. As a result, most of the bars are housed within restaurants or connected to them in some way, sometimes even bearing the same name. Once the kitchen closes, a few of them transform into nightclubs, so if you feel peckish after a few turns on the dance floor, you can always enjoy a snack at the bar

plate of charcuterie or cheese to go with them. If you're feeling particularly hungry, you can always try the dish of the day which comes in three versions – meat, fish or vegetarian. The list of wines sold by the glass changes daily and boasts no less than forty different varieties (by the bottle, however, there is ten times the choice). Wine lovers will also be impressed by the wonderful selection of champagnes, as well as the number of different spirits and schnapps on offer.

Akkurat
Horsngatan, 18 (B3/C3)
☎ **08 644 00 15**
Open Mon.-Fri. 11am-1am, Sat. noon-1am, Sun. 6pm-1am.

This specialist beer bar serves a huge range of whiskies and beers (18 draught and over 100 bottled varieties) in a cool and trendy atmosphere. It's a great place to relax after a hard day sightseeing. They also host live jazz and rock concerts at the weekends.

Kristallen
Blekingegatan, 40 (C4/D4)
☎ **08 556 09 090**
Open every day 5pm-1am.

This bar is adjacent to and forms part of the famous, historic Pelikan restaurant. It's definitely one of Södermalm's trendier venues. You could be forgiven for thinking you had popped round to visit the Addams family on entering this place, with its black walls, spiders and other ghostly and ghoulish features. It has a good atmosphere and is a favourite with local arty and

interesting types. The music can be rather loud but that's all part of the ambience.

Bistro Jarl
Birger Jarlsgatan (C1-2/D2)
☎ **08 611 76 30.**

This champagne bar, located on the chic Birger Jarlsgatan, is rather upmarket. You can dine here or simply enjoy a few glasses of bubbly from the impressive list on offer.

Lydmar Bar
Sturegatan, 10 (D1-2)
☎ **08 56 61 13 03**
Open every day 5pm-1am.

This bar is located in the lobby of Stockholm's trendiest hotel and is a stylish and immensely popular venue, with its dark and subtle decor. It's also one of the city's hottest night spots, where locals begin their evening's entertainment. If you're staying at the hotel, avoid arriving in the evening with all your luggage, when the foyer becomes an obstacle course filled with people dressed to the hilt, waiting for a

table in their favourite location. Most nights DJs play a range of music, but on some evenings you can enjoy lively soul or jazz concerts. It's worth dressing up a little to come here.

Operabaren
Operan
Karl XII Torget (D2)
☎ **08 676 58 09**
Open Mon.-Wed. 11.30am-1am, Thurs.-Fri. 11.30am-2am, Sat. 1pm-3am.

The Opera bar is just a few years short of its centenary, and little has changed since its doors first opened in 1905. The pure Art Nouveau decor, with its sculpted wood, leather benches and crystal chandeliers, is highly attractive and adds a touch of class to the atmosphere. Artists and business people mingle happily and enjoy a drink or meal at lunchtime and in the evenings.

Spy Bar
Birger Jarlsgatan, 20 (C1-2/D2)
Open Wed.-Sat. 10pm-5am.

The Spy Bar is housed in a lavish Stureplan apartment and is a favourite spot for young and loaded Stockholmers, as well as a number of its footballers and media stars. It isn't the easiest place to get into if you're not a well-known face, and is mainly members-only, but it's worth a try all the same.

Q-Lounge
Humlegårdsgatan, 14 (D2)
☎ **08 660 53 48**
Open every day 5pm-1am.

If you're in the mood for a spot of delicious, good value Thai food, then this is the place to come. If you've already eaten, however, you can still enjoy a drink or two at the bar and listen to the house DJ. The interior resembles a 1960s James Bond-style film set, with beige leather seating, dark brown walls and subtle lighting. The staff are particularly friendly and efficient, making it a pleasant spot to enjoy a relaxed evening.

Berns
Näckströmsgatan, 8 (D2)
☎ **08 566 322 22.**

Berns is an impressive bar located in the hotel of the same

name, and boasts a chic interior renovated by Sir Terence Conran. Sweden's young and trendy come here for a drink and mingle with hotel guests in the atmospheric bar, with its grand crystal chandeliers and attractive decor. In the evenings big name DJs entertain the crowds and occasionally they host live music concerts.

Laroy

Biblioteksgatan, 20 (D2)
☎ **08 545 037 00.**

Laroy is located on the ground floor of a magnificent early 20th-century triangular building, the Danelisuka Huset, with its flamboyant neo-Gothic architecture. It is home to a restaurant and bar, in a part of Stureplan where you'll find Stockholm's trendiest, designer-dressed youngsters. It's a cool venue and a good place to come for a glass of wine or champagne, without having to worry too much about wearing the latest labels.

Halv Trappa Plus Gård

Lästmakargatan, 3 (C2)
☎ **08 611 02 76.**

Here you can place your finger right on the pulse of Stockholm's nightlife. The bar is located above the restaurant (see p. 80) and features an inner courtyard surrounded by tall buildings. It's a popular venue on long (or to be more accurate – short) summer nights, but gets quite busy, so keep a hold of your glass.

Riche

Birger Jarlsgatan, 4 (C1-2/D2)
☎ **08 679 68 40.**

The atmosphere is quite relaxed at Riche, recently revamped by Jonas Bohlin. In a city obsessed

by youth, for once, you won't feel old if you're over 25. In fact, it's one of the few spots where thirty (or, heaven forbid, even forty) somethings feel comfortable and not 'over the hill'!

O-baren

Stureplan, at the entrance to the Sturegallerian (D2)
☎ **08 679 87 50.**

This is the Sturehof restaurant's second bar (see p. 82). To reach it, you have to cross the dining room and go up a few steps. It's a compulsory stop on every night owl's itinerary. Here you can admire the original interior designed by Jonas Bohlin, and enjoy the relaxed but ultra cool atmosphere. It's one of the city's hottest spots and is often full to bursting, but it's worth the crush.

East

Stureplan, 13 (D2)
☎ **08 611 49 59.**

The queue to get into East can be rather long sometimes, but it's worth putting up with it just to experience the rather unique atmosphere of this unusual Asian

restaurant (also see p. 80). It's one of the capital's most trendy hotspots and is always busy, loud and good fun. It's also popular with local Swedish celebrities – although it still remains fairly unpretentious.

CLUBBING

Café Opera

Operan
Karl XII Torget (entrance via Kungsträdgården) (D2)
☎ **08 676 58 07**
Open every day 5pm-3am.

This has been Scandinavia's number one night club for more than 20 years. The almost mythical Café Opera is adorned with beautiful ceiling frescoes painted by Vicke Andrén and a stunning Art Nouveau interior in which famous celebrities mingle with lesser mortals. This venue is a brasserie-style restaurant, bar, casino and nightclub all rolled into one, and in summer it spills out onto the terraces on the Kungsträd-gården. It's always buzzing and lively and you may have to queue to get in, but it's well worth the

wait. As in many of the city's night spots, there's a minimum entrance age of 23.

Sturecompagniet

Sturegatan, 4 (D1-2)
☎ **08 611 78 00**
Open Mon.-Wed. 11.30am-midnight, Thurs.-Sat. 11.30am-5am.

Situated not far from Stureplan, this huge nightclub is housed in an early 20th-century building, together with a small restaurant. There are three floors of bars and dancefloors, each with its own atmosphere and offering a variety of different music styles. The smallest and latest to open,

the Rainbow Room, is the most popular, with its mirrored walls, bright pink furry sofas and loud pumping music. You'll find all types here, from outlandish gay clubbers to Swedish soap stars who all come to dance the night away. It is quite hard to get in, however, and you may have to queue – unless, of course, you're a VIP.

Kharma

Sturegatan, 10 (D1-2)
☎ **08 662 04 65.**

It's trendy and cool at Kharma, and always full of young, trendy Stockholmers. Queueing is all

part of the experience, as it is in most of the cool clubs in town, but if you time it right, you may choose an evening when everything just gels perfectly – the clientele, the atmosphere and the music.

Seduction, Swedish-style

It's all done rather differently in Sweden, where the girls are definitely more liberated and very upfront about chatting up the guys. The boys, on the other hand, are a little more nervous and try to bolster their confidence with a drink or two. Their interest is often expressed so discreetly that it can be almost imperceptible – perhaps the subtle raising of an eyebrow will be your only clue. However, this signal of attraction should never be confused with a look of astonishment!

Fredsgatan 12
Fredsgatan, 12 (C2)
☎ 08 24 80 52.

You can only enjoy the unique atmosphere of Fredsgatan 12 during the summer. The restaurant owner, Danyel Couet (see p. 80), rents out the space during his holidays (for at least the whole of July), when it is transformed into one of Stockholm's busiest discos. The two terraces on the first floor of the Academy of Fine Arts, in which it is located, are turned into private, open-air bars offering spectacular views over Lake Mälaren and the Old Town. These terraces also provide a wonderful place from which to watch the sun rise at 3am. Disco al fresco – why not give it a try?

Mosebacke Etablissement
Mosebacke Torg, 3 (D3)
☎ 08 556 098 90.

Next to the Söder theatre, the Mosebacke Etablissement has a relaxed and arty feel. This music/cabaret venue stages themed evenings that range from jazz, swing and salsa to rock, folk and even stand-up comedy. There are two stages for live music and two dance floors, and in summer you can enjoy a drink or a bop on the terrace with its fabulous view over Djurgården. The tattoos and body piercing you'll come across here are a sharp contrast to the labels and expensive outfits you'll see at city centre venues.

Don't miss...

H ere is a selection of the top 11 sights to see in Stockholm that should be on any visitor's list.

3 SKANSEN

The oldest open-air museum in the world and one of the capital's most popular family attractions, Skansen is situated on the island of Djurgården and offers a fascinating journey through time and the chance to wander through the country-side – in the heart of the city.

1 HISTORISKA MUSEET

Opened in 1943, the History Museum is housed in an austere yellow building and traces the course of Swedish history from prehistoric times to the 18th century. Recently renovated, it houses some real treasures.

4 NORDISKA MUSEET

The Nordic museum – housed in a huge building constructed in Swedish Renaissance style at the start of the 20th century – is located at the entrance to Djurgården. The exhibits trace the story of daily life in Sweden through the centuries.

2 NATIONAL ART MUSEUM

Located on the island of Blasieholmen, the national museum has a majestic and striking waterfront façade. It is home to an impressive collection of fine and applied arts, including paintings, sculpture, textiles, furniture and silverware.

5 VASAMUSEET

The spectacular 17th-century warship displayed in the Vasa museum was raised along with thousands of objects from Stockholm's harbour in 1961. Commissioned by King Gustav II Adolf, it sank on its maiden voyage in 1628.

6 STORKYRKAN

Consecrated in 1306 and built by Birger Jarl as a replacement for the former church on the site, Storkyrkan stands on the highest point of the island known as Stadsholmen. It was renovated in the 15th century and sumptuously redecorated in the 17th century.

7 KUNGLIGA SLOTTET

The Royal Palace stands proudly on Slottsbacken hill and is one of the great symbols of the Swedish monarchy. Built in the 18th century, it is as equally impressive as Versailles or Buckingham Palace.

8 STADSHUSET

Built between 1911 and 1923, the City Hall is a landmark of modern Stockholm and a perfect example of the National Romantic style of architecture. It is home to the famous Golden Hall and Blue Hall where the annual Nobel Prize banquet is held.

9 DROTTNING-HOLM

Less than an hour by boat or car from the city centre, Drottningholm has been the permanent residence of the Swedish royal family since 1982, preferring to live in the peaceful park at the water's edge rather than in the austere Kungliga Slottet.

10 WALDERMAR-SUDDE

Prince Eugen, younger brother of King Gustav V, was a patron and lover of the arts, as well as a painter himself. He turned Waldemarsudde into an important artistic centre open to the public. It is surrounded by a wonderful garden that reaches down to the sea.

11 HAGAPARKEN

Less busy and touristy than Djurgården, Haga park is located at the gates of the city and is a haven of peace and nature, in which the inhabitants of Stockholm enjoy relaxing both in the summer and winter.

1 Historiska Museet

The Museum of National Antiquities traces Swedish history from 900 BC to AD 1600 and boasts the largest collection of artefacts from Sweden. Among the various highlights is the Gold Room with its magnificent medieval collections.

INFORMATION

**Historiska Museet
(see p. 52)
Narvavägen, 13-17
☎ 08 519 556 00
www.historiska.se
Metro Karlaplan or
Östermalmstorg
Open every day 11am-5pm
(15 May-14 Sept.),
Tue.-Sun. 11am-5pm (15
Sept.-14 May); late night
opening Thurs. to 8pm.
Entrance charge.**

GOLD, JEWELLERY AND COINS

This impressive collection is exhibited in a circular room, with a well in the middle into which you can throw your coins. The lavish display cabinets contain wonderful 5th-century gold collars, spirals, ingots, rings and other pieces of jewellery from the

Timboholm treasure, dating from AD 375-550. The gold hoard was discovered in 1904 and is thought to come from the smelting of Roman coins.

THE RELICS OF ST ELISABETH

The Gold Room houses a beautiful chalice containing the skull of St Elisabeth, its silver cover studded with precious

stones and carved motifs. There are also wonderful silver spoons, belt buckles and 15th-century brooches on display

THE MEDIEVAL ROOMS

The rooms on the first floor house collections of sacred gold artefacts, alongside crowns, jewellery and beautiful wooden statues from the 14th and 15th centuries.

THE VÄSTERGÖTLAND MEDIEVAL CHURCH

This reconstruction of a medieval church draws on elements from a variety of Swedish churches. There's also a collection of carved, painted wooden altarpieces from the 15th and 17th centuries.

② National Art Museum

Designed in the 19th century by the German architect Friedrich August Stüler, Sweden's largest art museum houses a magnificent collection of paintings, drawings, sculpture and applied arts, including a vast collection of porcelain. Inspired by the Venetian palaces, the building was intended to be an artistic delight in itself, with bas-reliefs on the façade illustrating the disciplines of sculpture, painting and architecture.

including fine works by Flemish artists from the 17th century, French painters from the 19th-20th centuries (Renoir, Degas, Gauguin etc.) and Swedish masters from the 17th-19th centuries.

GROUND FLOOR

The National Art Museum contains a workshop in which adults and children can try their hand at a variety of plastic arts. The resulting masterpieces are displayed in a small adjacent gallery.

Sculpture by Peterson

THE CAFÉ

After enjoying the exhibits, you can relax in the ground floor café (to the left of the entrance hall). Between 1994-95, Mats Wåhlin renovated the northern inner courtyard and turned it into a light and airy glass-roofed restaurant.

INFORMATION

National Art Museum (see p. 61)
Blasieholmshamnen (just before Skeppsholmsbron)
☎ 08 519 543 00
www.nationalmuseum.se
Metro Kungsträgården
Open Tue.-Thurs. 10am-9pm, Wed., Fri.-Sun. 10am-5pm, closed Mon. Entrance charge.

FIRST FLOOR

The first floor is devoted to the applied arts, with a permanent exhibition focusing on the past hundred years of Swedish design. Here you'll find everyday items that have become design icons, now selling for a considerable sum of money amongst collectors.

SECOND FLOOR

Lovers of painting and sculpture will enjoy the collection of 16,000 exhibits,

3 Skansen

For twenty years Artur Hazelius worked to build a collection destined to safeguard Sweden's traditional, popular and rural culture, and in 1891, with the arrival of industrialisation, he finally founded this open-air museum. It took ten years to complete and features 150 reconstructed buildings from many regions of Sweden, dating from the 16th century to the 1920s.

polar foxes and seals, as well as traditional livestock breeds and other domesticated animals.

A LIVING MUSEUM

During the day the houses are occupied by real people, dressed in traditional costume, who will tell you about how life used to be lived. You can see plenty of craftsmen busy at work, including weavers, spinners, glassblowers, blacksmiths, bakers, carpenters and shoemakers.

TOWN AND COUNTRY

The town quarters portray the lives of people from different social and professional backgrounds, whilst in the rural areas, you'll find farmsteads with livestock, displays of decorative crafts and demonstrations of butter and cheesemaking .

THE PARK AND THE ZOO

Sweden's flora and fauna are also much in evidence – visit the forest house, the rose garden and the small zoo, which is home to 70 different species of animals, including brown bears, reindeer, wolves,

INFORMATION

**Skansen (see p. 64)
Main entrance on
Djurgårdsslätten
☎ 08 442 80 00
www.skansen.se
Bus no. 44 or 47,
or ferry from Slussen
Park: open every day
(exc. 24 Dec.) 10am-8pm;
June-Aug. 10am-10pm;
Sept. 10am-5pm;
Historic houses: open
May-Sept. 11am-5pm;
Oct.-Apr. 11am-3pm;
Shop: open every day 11am-
5pm; Jan-Feb. 11am-4pm,
June-Aug. 11am-7pm.
Entrance charge.**

4 Nordiska Museet

The Nordiska Museet provides a valuable historical legacy, documenting everyday life in Sweden from the 16th century to the present day. In the entrance hall, the huge statue of the 16th-century Swedish king, Gustav Vasa, sculpted by Carl Milles, cuts an impressive figure. It's said that the sovereign's forehead was carved from the trunk of an oak tree that he planted himself.

furniture, including chairs, cupboards and chests, both plain and decorated, dating from 1500 to 1890. The clocks decorated with flower motifs are particularly worth a look.

TEMPORARY EXHIBITIONS

These exhibitions often celebrate the life and work of popular, contemporary

Swedish figures. A recent exhibition on the pop group, Abba, attracted plenty of nostalgic thirtysomethings.

INFORMATION

**Nordiska Museet
(see p. 65)
Djurgårdsvägen, 6
☎ 08 519 560 00
www.nordm.se
Metro Karlaplan
Open Tue.-Sun. 10am-5pm
(Wed. to 8pm), closed Mon.
Entrance charge.**

furniture, with such highlights as beautiful porcelain and silver tableware, displays of traditional Christmas fare and an interesting collection of Strindberg's paintings.

THE SECOND FLOOR

This floor is home to a collection of traditional

DAILY LIFE IN SWEDEN

The idea for a museum of Swedish cultural history was the brainchild of Artur Hazelius, creator of Skansen. Completed in 1907 and designed by the architect Isak Clason, it was originally intended to be four times its present size. The collections include traditional folk costumes, handicrafts, jewellery, toys and Swedish

5 Vasamuseet

To fight the Danes, King Gustav II Adolf commissioned the largest warship that had ever been built, the *Vasa*. It took three years to complete and was both heavily armed and lavishly adorned with gilded wooden sculptures and decoration. Its glory was short-lived, however, as it sank on its maiden voyage and languished on the seabed until finally being raised by a team of experts in 1961.

DAUNTING DIMENSIONS

The *Vasa* is 69 m (226 ft) long and six of its original ten sails have been preserved, their surface area measuring a staggering 1,275 sq m (13,724 sq ft). Thousands of oak trees were felled to make the ship's hull, the masts measured 50 m (164 ft) high and it was armed with over 60 canons.

THE DISASTER

On 10 August 1628, the *Vasa* set sail on its maiden voyage and fired a salute, but after only a few minutes the ship began to list and water gushed in through the open gunports. To the horror of the dignitaries and spectators gathered on the shore the mighty warship sank.

RAISING THE VASA

Attempts to raise the ship just after it sank were soon abandoned and it was not until 24 April 1961 that the *Vasa* finally broke the surface. To everyone's amazement, it was in excellent condition, having been preserved in silt for over three hundred years.

JEWEL IN THE CROWN

To maintain its preservation, the ship is kept at a constant temperature and is displayed in semi-darkness. The *Vasa* is surrounded by viewing platforms, and there's a fascinating exhibition which recreates life on board this magnificent vessel.

INFORMATION

Vasamuseet (see p. 67)
Galärvarnet
☎ 08 519 548 00
www.vasamuseet.se
Bus no. 44 or 47,
or ferry from Slussen
Open every day mid-June
to mid-Aug. 9.30am-7pm,
mid-Aug. to mid-June
10am-5pm, (Wed. to 8pm).
Entrance charge.

6 Storkyrkan

Birger Jarl is thought to have built the original church on this site in the 13th century. Having undergone a series of reconstructions over the centuries, it eventually became the city's cathedral. The exterior is somewhat austere, despite the Baroque-inspired façade, but there are some exceptional treasures inside.

amazing work of art offers a fascinating depiction of Gamla Stan in the 16th century.

SPECIAL CEREMONIES

The marriage of the current Swedish sovereign was celebrated in the cathedral in 1976. Each year the winners of the Nobel Prize give a speech here during a special ceremony.

ST GEORGE AND THE DRAGON

The impressive oak statue of St George and the Dragon is the work of Bernt Notke of Lübeck, commissioned to sculpt the saint in celebration of Sten Sture the Elder's victory over King Christian of Denmark. A 19th-century bronze replica of the statue stands in Köpmantorget square.

THE TREASURES

The flamboyant, wooden pulpit was carved by Burchardt Precht. The seven-stemmed bronze candelabra, which is 4 m (13 ft) high, dates from the 15th century, and the stunning black and silver altarpiece was donated in the 17th century by the royal adviser, Johan Adler Salvius.

THE PARHELION PAINTING

The stunning Parhelion painting dates from the 16th century and is attributed to Urban. Commissioned by the great reformer Olaus Petri, it portrays an extraordinary phenomenon in the skies over Stockholm on 20 April 1535, when six halos appeared resembling false suns. This

INFORMATION

Storkyrkan (see p. 41)
Trångsund, 1
☎ **08 723 30 21**
Metro Gamla Stan
**Open every day 9am-4pm
(to 6pm 14 May-15 Sept.).
Free entrance.
Guided tours available
1 July-19 Aug (fee charged).**

7 Kungliga Slottet

Commissioned by King Karl XI to design the Royal Palace, architect Nicodemus Tessin the Younger drew inspiration from the Italian Baroque style. The palace was built to replace the former Tre Kronor (Three Crowns) fortress, destroyed by fire in 1697, and was completed in 1754. It houses the staterooms, the Treasury and the royal stables.

with its beautiful silver throne, a gift from Magnus Gabriel de la Gardie to Queen Kristina on her coronation in 1650. It's protected by a blue canopy embroidered in gold (the Swedish national colours), and stands opposite the parliamentary benches.

THE PALACE APARTMENTS

The Royal Palace is the official residence of the royal family, although they prefer to live in Drottningholm castle, and Carl XVI Gustaf hosts official receptions here. At the heart of the palace, built around a square courtyard, you can visit the Banqueting rooms, the Bernadotte and Guest apartments, the Hall of State, the Royal Chapel and the Apartments of the Orders of Chivalry. The grand staircase is very impressive, along with the magnificent ceiling painted in the 19th century in honour of Moder Svea (Mother Sweden).

THE KARL XI GALLERY

One of Sweden's Baroque treasures, with wonderful decorative features painted on the ceiling and around the windows, and 17th- and 18th- century objets d'art. The beautiful ivory and amber pieces come from Queen Hedwig Eleonora's collection.

THE HALL OF STATE

Make sure you visit The Hall of State on the ground floor

INFORMATION
Kungliga Slottet
(see p. 40)
Slottsbacken
(entrance tickets on Högvaktsterrassen)
☎ **08 402 61 30**
www.royalcourt.se
Metro Gamla Stan
Open Tue.-Sun. noon-3pm (1 Sept.-14 May), every day 10am-4pm (14 May-31 Aug.).
Entrance charge.

8 Stadshuset

Stockholm's City Hall stands majestically on the shores of Lake Mälaren, with its distinctive brick façade and square tower. Built between 1911 and 1923 by Ragnar Östberg, the Stadshuset is a fine example of the Swedish National Romantic style and one of the city's most symbolic landmarks.

THE BLUE HALL AND THE CITIZENS COURTYARD

The Italian Renaissance provided the inspiration for the design of these two *piazze*. Every year on the 10th of December the Nobel Prize banquet is held in the Blå Hallen (The Blue Hall) – blue in name only – which can hold up to 1,300 delegates.

THE GOLDEN HALL

Drinks before the Nobel Prize banquet are served in the Golden Hall, with its stunning mosaic frescoes encrusted with gold leaf. The 'Queen of Lake Mälaren' (representing Stockholm), is depicted on the back wall receiving a tribute from the East and the West.

THE COUNCIL CHAMBER

Town council meetings held in this chamber are open to the public. The ceiling is really impressive, comprising rows of narrow wooden beams, resembling the upturned hull of a Viking ship.

THE FRENCH ROOM

Civil weddings are regularly performed in this prestigious room, decorated with beautiful 17th-century Beauvais tapestries. The participants can choose from two services, the shortest of which lasts less than a minute.

INFORMATION

Stadshuset (see p. 62)
Hantverkargatan, 1
☎ 08 508 290 58
Metro Rådhuset or
T-Centralplan
Open every day (except
Christmas Eve, Christmas
Day and New Year's Day)
Guided tours only, 10am
and noon (plus 11am and
2pm, 1 June-31 Aug.).
Tower open every day
1am-4.30pm, May-Sept.
Entrance charge.

9 Drottningholm

The construction of the fabulous Drottningholm estate began in 1662. It was built for King Karl X's widow Eleonora, and stands on the leafy shores of Lake Mälaren. One of the wings of the palace provides a permanent home for the royal family and the grounds include several gardens, a Chinese Pavilion and a theatre. Drottningholm is an Unesco world heritage site.

THE PALACE

The magnificent palace stands at the end of an avenue lined with trees and statues. Before heading off to explore the apartments, take a look at the room near the entrance porch,

housing King Oskar III's 18th-century collection of porcelain, and decorated almost entirely in blues tiles. Plates and other decorative earthenware items are also displayed on the walls. The palace's grand imposing staircase takes up one third of the entire building, and the wonderful trompe l'oeil marble walls feature Baroque stuccoes by Giovanni and Carlo Carove, illustrating Queen Hedwig Eleonora's wardrobes.

QUEEN LOVISA ULRIKA'S LIBRARY

This is one of the highlights of the palace. The architect Jean Eric Rehn was commissioned to design the room in 1760 and the fabulous rock crystal pendant chandeliers were gifts from France in the 1700s. The shelves are crammed full of books in different languages and a collection of miniature statues in white marble adorn the tables.

THE CHAPEL

The octagonal-shaped chapel is situated at one end of the palace. Furnished with plain wooden benches, painted white, the atmosphere is quite light, if a little austere. Classical music concerts are held here and are open to the public.

THE THEATRE

Queen Lovisa Ulrika commissioned the construction

INFORMATION

Drottningholm
(see pp. 72-73)
www.royalcourt.se
Metro Brommaplan then
any of the buses
numbered 301-323,
or by boat from Klara
Mälarstrand quay.

The Royal Palace
☎ 08 402 62 80
Open May-Aug. every day
10am-4.30pm; Sept.
every day noon-3.30pm;
Oct.-Apr. Sat.-Sun.
noon-3.30pm.
Entrance charge.

Court Theatre
☎ 08 759 04 06
Open May, every day noon-
4.30pm; June, 11am-
4.30pm; Sept., 1-3.30pm.
Guided tours only.
Entrance charge.

The Guards Tent
Open mid-June to mid-
Aug. every day noon-4pm.
Entrance free.

The Chinese Pavilion
☎ 08 402 62 70
Open May-Aug. every day
11am-4.30pm, Sept. every
day noon-3.30pm.
Entrance charge.

of the theatre, designed by
Carl Fredrik Adelcrantz, in
1762. The royal guests used to
sit on ordinary seats amongst
the audience, while the royal
mistresses remained incognito
within the enclosed boxes.
The building is simple and
functional, made out of wood
with a plaster frontage and
interior papier-mâché
supports. The 18th-century
special effects and hand-driven
machinery are very impressive
and the stage sets are a perfect
example of the art of illusion.
This is Europe's oldest
functioning theatre and home
to an annual summer festival.

THE ENGLISH GARDENS

Within the extensive palace
grounds you'll find the
Chinese Pavilion and the
Guard's Tent. In 1753, King
Adolf Fredrik built the small
pavilion for Lovisa Ulrika as a
birthday gift, demonstrating

the 18th-century fascination
with the Orient. Each room
is a delight, in particular the
embroidery room with its
mural wall panels embroidered
by Queen Lovisa Ulrika and
her ladies in waiting. Nearby
are a number of smaller
pavilions, including one that
houses a dining room, where
the King could dine in peace.

10 Waldermarsudde

The estate of Prince Eugen (1865-1945) is situated to the south of the island of Djurgården and is, in effect, the gateway to the archipelago. The terraces of the impressive 'English' gardens lead down to the sea and are full of sculptures. At the far end stands an 18th-century linseed oil mill, with an eye-catching red wood and copper exterior.

the house is open to the public for guided tours (in Swedish) and at the end of the visit, you can enjoy a drink or snack in the kitchen. In summer, classical music concerts are held at the house (programme available from the Tourist Office, Hamngatan, 27).

A PRINCE AMONGST BOTANISTS

Prince Eugen's interest in the natural world began as a child. He loved to spend time walking or painting in Waldemarsudde, which he acquired at the beginning of the 20th century, and installed his studio in the winter garden, from where he would gaze out across the sea.

THE PRIVATE APARTMENTS

The prince commissioned the architect Ferdinand Boberg to design him a home where he could also store his art collection. Restored in 2001,

THE GALLERY

Prince Eugen was an avid art collector and built his own gallery, now a museum, on the site of the former winter garden. He displayed his sculptures and paintings in the huge exhibition spaces, wisely protected from any potential damage by sunlight.

INFORMATION

Prins Eugens Walder-marsudde (See p. 66)
Prins Eugens Väg, 6
☎ **08 545 837 00**
www.waldermarsudde.com
Bus no. 47 or tram no. 7
Open Tue.-Sun. 11am-5pm
(Thurs. to 8pm); Park
open daily, all year round.
Guided tour in English:
Tues.-Fri. 3pm (June-Aug.).
Entrance charge.

Hagaparken

11

Enjoy a relaxing walk in the wonderful Haga Park, created in the 18th century by King Gustav III to house his royal palace. It was intended to rival Versailles in magnificence but was never completed. The large park, covering many hectares, lies on the shores of the peaceful Brunnsviken bay where many pleasure boats are moored.

Rome. There are also a number of grottoes and fountains scattered among the trees.

A TOUCH OF THE EXOTIC

At the Fjärils and Fågelhuset, butterflies and exotic birds fly freely in a lush tropical rainforest environment, housed in a succession of glasshouses. There are also botanical gardens and a Japanese garden.

as well as the superb library with its plaster medallion featuring the king's profile.

FOUNTAINS AND MORE PAVILIONS

As you take a walk through the gardens you may come across the charming pagoda-style Chinese temple with its impressive dragons, or the Ekotemplet, inspired by Ancient Roman art which the king discovered on a trip to

GUSTAV III'S PAVILION

This splendid pavilion was built by the king as a temporary home while his palace was being constructed. Behind the yellow facade, the interior, designed by Louis Masreliez, is a perfect example of the late Gustavian style. The glass-walled dining room offers a wonderful view over the gardens and the water,

INFORMATION

Hagaparken (see p. 70)
Gustav III's Pavilion:
☎ 08 402 61 30
www.royalcourt.se
Bus no. 52 or 515
Open 15 May–31 Aug.
Tue.–Sun. noon–3pm;
Sept. Sat.–Sun. noon–3pm.
(guided tours only).
Entrance charge.
Haga Parkmuseum
Open 15 May–31 Aug.
Tue.–Sun. noon–4pm.
Free entrance.

Conversion tables for clothes shopping

Women's sizes

Shirts/dresses

UK	USA	EUROPE
8	6	36
10	8	38
12	10	40
14	12	42
16	14	44
18	16	46

Sweaters

UK	USA	EUROPE
8	6	44
10	8	46
12	10	48
14	12	50
16	14	52

Shoes

UK	USA	EUROPE
3	5	36
4	6	37
5	7	38
6	8	39
7	9	40
8	10	41

Men's sizes

Shirts

UK	USA	EUROPE
14	14	36
$14^{1/2}$	$14^{1/2}$	37
15	15	38
$15^{1/2}$	$15^{1/2}$	39
16	16	41
$16^{1/2}$	$16^{1/2}$	42
17	17	43
$17^{1/2}$	$17^{1/2}$	44
18	18	46

Suits

UK	USA	EUROPE
36	36	46
38	38	48
40	40	50
42	42	52
44	44	54
46	46	56

Shoes

UK	USA	EUROPE
6	8	39
7	9	40
8	10	41
9	10.5	42
10	11	43
11	12	44
12	13	45

More useful conversions

1 centimetre	0.39 inches	1 inch	2.54 centimetres
1 metre	1.09 yards	1 yard	0.91 metres
1 kilometre	0.62 miles	1 mile	1. 61 kilometres
1 litre	1.76 pints	1 pint	0.57 litres
1 gram	0.035 ounces	1 ounce	28.35 grams
1 kilogram	2.2 pounds	1 pound	0.45 kilograms

This guide was written by **Anne Desnos**, with assistance from
Élodie Louvet, **Virginie Mahieux**, **Jean-Pierre Marenghi** and
Magali Vidal
Cover: **Thibault Reumaux**
Design: **Chrystel Arnould**
UK edition translated and edited by **JMS Books llp** and
Sofi Mogensen
Additional research and assistance: **Christine Bell**

We would like to thank Caroline Lilja-Grilly, Helena Nahon and all the
staff at the Swedish Tourist Offices in Paris and Stockholm for their
invaluable advice and ready assistance in the preparation of this guide.
We would also like to thank Andrea Salvi of SAS airlines.

We have done our best to ensure the accuracy of the information contained in this
guide. However, addresses, phone numbers, opening times etc. inevitably do
change from time to time, so if you find a discrepancy please do let us know.
You can contact us at: HachetteTravel@philips-maps.co.uk or write to us at the
address below.

Hachette Travel Guides provide independent advice. The authors and compilers
do not accept any remuneration for the inclusion of any addresses in these guides.

Please note that we cannot accept any responsibility for any loss, injury or
inconvenience sustained by anyone as a result of any information or advice
contained in this guide.

Photo acknowledgements

Inside pages:
All the photographs in this guide were taken by **Nicolas Edwige**, with the exception of those on the following pages:
Stockholm Tourist Office: Jens Thuresson p. 14 (b.c.); **Tina Buckman** p. 15 (b.r.); **Richard Ryan** p. 15 (c.c., t.),
p. 107 (t), p. 121 (t.r.), p. 122 (b.), p. 123 (b.).
Photothèque Hachette: p. 28 (c.l.); p. 34 (b.l.)

Cover
Nicolas Edwige, with the exception of the figures: © **PhotoDisc, Andersen Ross** (t.c.), © **Image Bank,
Werner Bokelberg** (b.c.); © **PhotoDisc, Ryan McVay** (b.r.)
Back cover:
Nicolas Edwige

Illustrations
Virginia Pulm

First published in the United Kingdom in 2002 by Hachette UK

© English Translation Hachette UK 2002
© Hachette Livre (Hachette Tourisme) 2002

Distributed in the United States of America by Sterling Publishing Co., Inc.
387 Park Avenue South, New York, NY 10016-8810

A CIP catalogue for this book is available from the British Library

ISBN 0 54008 318 6

Hachette Travel Guides, c/o Philip's, 2–4 Heron Quays, London E14 4JP

Printed and bound in Slovenia by DELO tiskarna by arrangement with Preševrnova družba

HACHETTE TRAVEL GUIDES

A GREAT WEEKEND IN …

Amsterdam	1 84202 145 1
Barcelona	0 54008 323 2
Berlin	1 84202 061 7
Brussels	1 84202 017 X
Budapest	0 54008 274 0
Dublin	1 84202 096 X
Florence	0 54008 322 4
Lisbon	1 84202 011 0
London	1 84202 168 0
Madrid	1 84202 095 1
Naples	1 84202 016 1
New York	0 54008 321 6
Paris	1 84202 001 3
Prague	1 84202 000 5
Rome	1 84202 169 9
Seville	0 54008 275 9
Venice	1 84202 018 8
Stockholm	0 54008 318 6
Vienna	1 84202 026 9

ROUTARD

Indulge your taste for travel with the ultimate food, drink and accommodation guides for the independent traveller.

Andalucia & Southern Spain	1 84202 028 5
Athens & the Greek Islands	1 84202 023 4
Belgium	1 84202 022 6
North Brittany	1 84202 020 X
California, Nevada & Arizona	1 84202 025 0
Canada	1 84202 031 5
Cuba	1 84202 062 5
Ireland	1 84202 024 2
Paris	1 84202 027 7
Provence & the Côte d'Azur	1 84202 019 6
Rome & Southern Italy	1 84202 021 8
Thailand	1 84202 029 3

VACANCES

Colourful, information-packed, leisure and activity guides. Hundreds of suggestions for things to do and sights to see.

Alsace	1 84202 167 2
The Ardèche	1 84202 161 3
The Basque Country	1 84202 159 1
Brittany	1 84202 007 2
Catalonia	1 84202 099 4
Corsica	1 84202 100 1
The Dordogne & Périgord	1 84202 098 6
French Alps	1 84202 166 4
Languedoc-Roussillon	1 84202 008 0
Normandy	1 84202 097 8
Poitou-Charentes	1 84202 009 9
Provence & the Côte d'Azur	1 84202 006 4
Pyrenees & Gascony	1 84202 015 3
South West France	1 84202 014 5